Act V, Scene I

Act V, Scene I

poems

Stanley Moss

Seven Stories Press

New York / Oakland / Liverpool

SEVEN STORIES PRESS
140 Watts Street
New York, NY 10013
www.sevenstories.com

Distributed by PENGUIN RANDOM HOUSE

LIBRARY OF CONGRESS CATALOGING-IN-PUBLICATION DATA

Names: Moss, Stanley, author.
Title: Act V, Scene I : poems / Stanley Moss.
Description: New York : Seven Stories Press, [2020]
Identifiers: LCCN 2020016114 (print) | LCCN 2020016115 (ebook) | ISBN 9781644210307 (trade paperback) | ISBN 9781644210314 (ebook)
Subjects: LCGFT: Poetry.
Classification: LCC PS3563.O885 A65 2020 (print) | LCC PS3563.O885 (ebook) | DDC 811/.54--dc23
LC record available at https://lccn.loc.gov/2020016114
LC ebook record available at https://lccn.loc.gov/2020016115

Printed in the USA.

9 7 5 3 1 2 4 6 8

Acknowledgements

We are grateful to Carcanet Press for permitting us to reprint poems that originally appeared in *God Breaketh Not All Men's Hearts Alike: New and Selected Poems 1948-2019.*

We also wish to thank the following journals: *PN Review (UK), Times Literary Supplement, The New Yorker, The Nation, Notre Dame Review, Poetry (Chicago), Eco Theo (Hawaii), Harvard Review, Tikkun, Literary Imagination, The American Poetry Review, Piano, Manoa,* etc.

These poems were written in 2018, 2019, and the first half of 2020, when the printer was struck by the global pandemic. However, my writing continues unscathed, except for my old and new virtues and vices. —SM

Cover painting: *The Dream of Human Life*, by Alessandro Allori

Contents

Before the Curtain

Act V, Scene I   13
Wandering   15
January 2nd, 2018   17
Yusef Komunyakaa   19
That's That and Not That   20
What's Left   24
For Laurence Olivier, with Years of Gratitude   25
I Choose to Write a Poem   28
Water Music   29
I'm Sorry   32
Mishearing   33
Frivolity   35
Pub Crawl   37
A March 3, 2020 Birthday Card, Mailed
    September 1, 2019 to Michael Schmidt   39
Random   41
They Plow Their Father's Field   43
Zigong, Salt City of China   44
China Poem   45

Stage Left, Stage Right

Joy   49
Easy Does It   51
Wishing   54
O Beautiful O Beautiful Girl   57
Second Look   59

It's My Turn 60

Spit Tune 62

For W.S. Merwin 64

Have a Heart, Brain, Kidney, and Lung 66

Happy Birthday Letter to Rebecca Berlow 67

Xmas Carol 70

Snood of Garlic 71

Vertigo 71

Bedtime Story 72

Exit

Postamble 77

A Lesson 78

Ode to Stella Halkyard, Rylands Librarian Soon to Retire 80

Snake in a Basket of Groceries 82

Whimper 85

Elegy for Emily Fragos's Cat Sue 85

Twins 87

To Alexander Fu Who Wanted to Be a Cosmologist 88

Gaudy Ode 89

Requiem for Ice 90

Sunny Day 92

Ode to a Snapshot 94

Who Am I to Say? 96

These Days 97

A True Berlin Short Story 100

Low A 100

50th Anniversary Poem for Cella and Norman Manea 101

Pocket Mirror 103

Galileo, Who Recanted, Told Me the Truth 105

Ode to New York City Trees 106

Poem for Naomi 107

I Admire a Brave Ant on my Tablecloth 108

Forest Fires 110

A Smiling Understanding 112

Happiness 113

Christmas 2019 114

A Touch 117

Tuning Up 118

Early Poem That Disappeared 120

Poem With Two Titles 121

Not Reading or Writing, Waiting 123

Unknown Reason For 125

Scuttlebutt 126

Manservant 128

Happy Holiday 129

My History of Laughter 130

Three 135

Pasture 138

Resemblance 140

Pandemic: Wear Gloves and a Mask 142

Pratfall 143

Ode to an Antique Boy 146

Dieu est le seul etre qui, pour régner,
n'ait meme pas besoin dexister.
                —Charles Baudelaire

Whatever their personal faith,
all poets, as such,
are polytheists.
                —W.H. Auden

The wilderness and the solitary place shall be glad for them;
and the desert shall rejoice, and blossom as the rose.
                —Isaiah 35:1

A life in which the gods are not invited isn't worth living.
                —Robert Calasso

I

Before the Curtain

Act V, Scene I

Stanley: Anything that is, is company,
　　　a dog a stone a spoon a book windows,
　　　anything inside or outside,
　　　　　meditations, lullabies, and requiems
　　　sung for the first time.
　　　I listen to space, colliding clouds
　　　chance meetings, bumpings-into.
　　　Everything stops but changing weather.

　　　Clouds and smoke don't have the same gods.
　　　Look for your twin and anti-twin,
　　　there's nothing in the world not like you.
　　　Like Kafka, build a castle of dry leaves
　　　every leaf like your eyebrows and ears.
　　　Well water proves the existence of thirst,
　　　everything has an opposite,
　　　death still the opposite of everything.

　　　Bakeries across France are vanishing,
　　　in their place baguette vending machines.
　　　Words like *baguette* came to be needed,
　　　the bark of a tree, a dog, a French barque,
　　　words age and are invented, God knows,
　　　because there's a need to give and receive.
　　　A fool complains a need to rhyme is a necessity.
　　　Poetry's better proof of the meaning of words

　　　than a dictionary. Still, hats off to the OED.
　　　What was I waiting for?
　　　There were colors before there were paintings.
　　　What came first, the obvious or the obscure,

obvious love before obscure affection?
Certainly mother love before father love,
whole wheat before pumpernickel.
In Elizabethan years, plays were written not to be staged.

I don't want to say "that is the answer" and fall asleep
after my sudden disappearance, when I'm laughing ashes.
Among sitting friends, someone repeats my last words:
"May there be abundant peace from Heaven."
Let them say that he saved a few damned souls,
his dust made a deer mouse sneeze, and he wrote,
for his own religious entertainment,
Act V, Scene I.

Wandering

I will live longer than a cloud
that is never in God's image.
Sometimes in the sky I see sleeping sheep,
their heads against their chests.
I'm a cloudy man in a corduroy sky-blue suit.
I do not practice Quietism.
I took a seminar in the poetry of transfiguration
and annunciation from Fra Angelico.
I bought pigments from a messenger
of the Lord along the Arno:
cinnabar red, and snail mucus purple
that Virgil said was the color of the soul.
Who am I to follow Virgil's teaching? But I do.
I remember Rembrandt's bodies, nothing purple,
he painted shades of the soul.
I have a wise etching: Rembrandt's Good Samaritan
with a wounded, suffering man Christ saved.
In the foreground, a dog defecating.
My dogs visit my neighbor's barn and so do I.
I see a Catholic woman milking a beloved goat.

For a lark, I paint my soul in purple on oak panel:
a purple forest, waterfalls, my old friend the Tiber.
Trees are not liars. Leaves tell the truth
like every other leaf before them.
Heaven with its fires may fall down next winter.
Planets, suns, and stars,
black holes, emptiness may fall down.
I want to live longer than a cloud, till I
can't mourn the beloved dead any longer.
I tell myself *festina lente*, rush slowly,
from your farm take the turnpike, the shortcut

through apple country, smiling at grief
between Salt Point and Poughkeepsie, then follow
your clouds around the world. Whatever the weather,
I linger here and there. I think of Faust with his dog,
but I am an earthling,
neither Heaven or Hell is satisfactory.
On the last day of the world, I will plant a blue spruce,
proof I'm mourning a dead friend.

January 2ⁿᵈ, 2018

> "We have no lasting friends, no lasting enemies, only lasting interests."
> —Winston Churchill

"Abandon Ship," I said to myself
for no reason
just a little before a late sunrise.
Why do I say two words that frighten me,
a command I was never given except by myself?
In a drill, we rehearsed the possibility
three score and thirteen years ago.

In icy January 1959
at a place of contemplation
the convent of Santo Domingo El Antiguo
in Toledo, Spain, a black veiled nun
greeted me through iron bars, said
"Quien pasa un Enero, vive un año entero,"

      * *

January 2nd 2018
last night I made a resolution:
This year no friend will die.
Five days passed. On the seventh of January,
Daniel, my friend for 60 years,
Eugene, my friend for 50, died on the same day.
In the evening of that day,
I heard a third friend, a poet
refused a tablespoon of coffee
he just asked for, stumbling for words—
he could not swallow or get out of bed.
When we first met I was nineteen,

17

he was buying a girlfriend a pretty bottle
of perfume, *Evening in Paris.*
My first words to him in a pharmacy-bookstore:
"Every whore in Paris wears that."
8th of January, about noon
his wife called and said, "Aaron's dead,
eight days after his 92nd birthday."

January 10, Laren called from Germany,
"Yusef had a stroke, his right side and left arm
are paralyzed." I called him, we chattered,
he did not say, "Goodbye," he said, "Man, keep the faith."
January 22, Christopher emailed me from Tangier,
"Stanley,
I'm sorry to tell you Bill Jordan just died."
February 1, at a party I was told,
"Arthur died yesterday."
He was my oldest friend.
At seventeen, we joined the Navy,
bunked together. Later he lost a leg,
had six children, twenty-nine grandchildren last count.
He had the heartiest laugh I ever heard,
it rocked the ship. I loved him.

I do not abandon ship, I bail with my hands.
I'm not afraid to say I don't know.
I wish the world a Happy New Year!

Yusef Komunyakaa

Dear Yusef, after a stroke
not of an oar or swimmer,
you're paralyzed on the right side,
part of both arms. They're attaching
a pacemaker to your heart right now.
It should keep your heart beating,
so you will get off the table into a bed.
My heart feels funny, guess my heart's praying,
but I don't pray.

Life is suddenly a battlefield,
the world needs you more than anyone.
I don't want to write: "more than anyone I know."
You have given us holy thoughts,
your heart and intelligence have constructed
a free nation for all, beauty for all
like rice and sweet potatoes.
The Greeks say, I know, "A poet is a maker."
I don't know the Greek word for *cook*.
I think poems are not made,
they're cooked, or eaten raw.

God invented us and green poison ivy.
Simple fact, it's absolutely senseless doing evil.
God, if you exist, are you grateful?
I would be grateful if you grabbed me
by the balls and pulled me up to heaven,
only if I can tell stories of a child murdered.
What would Mary have done if she strangled Jesus—
man, you know from experience:
she would have hanged herself. Now this.

That's That and Not That

1.
I'm on my way to hell
claiming I heard conversations
between Allah and Yahweh.
They spoke mixed Arabic and Hebrew,
international underground English:
"Human beings look more like me than you.
They praise me more often,
I'm praised 5 times a day,
you just morning and night, and on the Sabbath.
You've got prayers for the dead,
the new moon, every damn thing."
I heard Yahweh answer,
"Wind and spirit in Hebrew are the same word."

That's that and not that.
I am the Groucho Marx Professor of Theology
at the College of Hard Knocks,
I give a Red Sea plus to a liar's thesis
"The God's Honest Truth."
My lecture: Yahweh speaks Snow, Rain,
Sunset, Drought, Flood, Bird Call, and Whippoorwill.
Yahweh clears His throat with Lightning.
Lightning strikes this old intruder—there's a pause,
I thunder words:
"After death, life's not silent."

*   *   *

I became a man,
I memorized misbegotten conversations.
Still I'm ignorant as I was inside my mother's womb,
where I kicked, laughed, but never wept—

till I was born, given light.
I have faith in Silence.
I find it a discomfort to be vague,
the text of a great Arabic poet reveals,
"Life by its nature is absent.
Time, in all its rotten presence,
is no more than a joke."
Vegetarian, Abu Al-Maʿarri
never made a "pagan journey."

Boys and girls,
I believe in mysteries,
what the Greeks called music.
I offer an olive on a toothpick.
My friend said, "A violin is a replica of the soul."
I vow, nosey, I heard Yahweh and Allah
speaking alone, each to Himself,
praying as Jesus did in John 17.
Is Paradise a theater, never dark? I want,
I want to hear Allah and Yahweh sing—
they must be full throated
bass, baritone, mezzosoprano, coloratura.
Allah and Yahweh do not sing to me.
They speak to the seen and unseen
because nothing is speechless,
they have laughing conversations with pebbles,
darkness, every ant hill, the Himalayas.
By the way, my Stone is better than my French,
I speak a little Waterfall with a New York drawl.

2.

Lord help me
if there's aftermath, religious wars after death,
dead souls against dead souls.
Kindness without flesh bleeds to death,
because, because… no matter.
I named my motorboat *Because*.
Some like to play football, tennis, chess,
I like to play this. I hear sacred music,
a lone flute challenging a cradle cithara.
No matter, "The only question is the existence
or non-existence of God" Dostoyevsky wrote.
I see from a mountaintop two naked witches
flying on a broomstick across a valley,
my pretty teachers—
above them a horned owl with stretched out wings.
Far below are people the size of ants.
I must brush up on my Sumerian.

3.

From the balcony of a three-star hotel in Eilat,
I hold my head still, moving only my eyes.
Straight ahead I see across the waters Arabia,
eyes left Jordan— eyes right Egypt,
Saint Catherine's Monastery.
I hear noise for the Lord:
an Arab says *Jerusalem is a Moslem city*,
then he says *Fuck off* in Hebrew, that has no such word.
A Jew says *Fuck off* in Arabic, that has no such word.
Peace is taxi drivers arguing in the street.
Forgiveness began when Joseph forgave his brothers.

I hand you this slice of lemon pie on a paper plate,
my pathetic argument for peace in the Middle East.
In Vietnam, my friend Frances
saw war through the window of a clinic
a dog running with a human baby leg in its mouth.
My front door is always open for God
to come to supper.

What's Left

What's left, not far across the world,
war leaves a Yemeni child starving,
a ten-year-old boy weighs thirty pounds.
What can I offer him to eat?
One day the sky will be bread,
the earth bread, everything between
the makings of my sandwich.
I eat my sandwich now:
the Great Wall of China
gets caught between my teeth.
My mother said "Don't talk
with food in your mouth."
I stop talking now.
The boy's mother walks on her knees
across a fig tree minefield.

For Laurence Olivier, with Years
of Gratitude

1.

I do not speak at the beginning
but the end of a breath.
My first night on a public stage,
not having the money for the toll bridge or subway,
I swam across the Thames and East River.
I was an Ancient Greek naked actor,
I played tragedy and comedy, the attendance
by law only free Athenian men.

Like any child, I acted,
most stop in their teens,
let the curtain fall forever.
They dream their own dreams,
while actors spend their lives
acting out the dreams of others.

2.

I sometimes explode a spoken word.
I never gabble. In Shakespeare's day,
a boy actor played Cordelia and The Fool.
I could not recognize myself
when I took off my makeup,
an old dog inspecting yesterday's bones.
I breathed into the nostrils of the character.
Sometimes I chose to be in the wrong place
at the wrong time. I smell the play,
I played Iago for laughs, sweet
and charming, every performance like music,
always different. I lived the life,
body and soul, of a fourth spear onstage.

"Reading may be better than nothing,
but it is not the same as feeling and
understanding Shakespeare's great lines
through the interpretations of an actor."

Eugene O'Neill would not talk to his wife
for weeks when he was writing.
William Wyler said, "If you want to shock
an audience, bore them a little first."
Trying to learn at the same time words and accents
is the folly of my life, not the *folie* Baudelaire.
I play Mr. Nothing now,
I don't upstage an actor anymore
by eating grapes during his great speeches.
I ask myself for the impossible,
the only way I can play the scene,
hanging from the chandelier.
Without a moment's hesitation I reply,
"Of course, no problem."

3.

In the United Kingdom I'm an American,
a foreigner who learned the language too carefully.
I don't think I am a very good crowd.
Truth is, I always write to be read out loud,
separated by a holy and profane distance,
from the pit and the gentles.
At the Old Vic, angel and virgin, the audience was reborn
from a pollen of words, from lily to the ear.

Perhaps lonely,
Laurence Olivier wrote— Churchill agreed,
"I don't think we could have won the war
without . . . 'Once more, unto the breach'
somewhere in our soldiers' hearts."

4.

Off to the Old Vic to see whatever, I caught
the last performance of Olivier on stage—
a Scottish labor leader in Griffiths' *The Party.*
Then he set sail for the movies and TV.
I wish I could see what he left
on the cutting room floor.
According to Brecht, without a curtain,
"You can make a fresh start with your final words."
I am a soothsayer, three witches,
I cauldron my blaspheming liver.
Jeremiah lamenting the fall of Jerusalem,
I don't have the nails required for a crucifixion.
I count my fingernails and toenails out loud.
I fly away, my life an opening and closing book.
I don't care if you can't tell my book
from a butterfly or a blackbird.
The play goes on in darkness, mostly exits.

I never was a sleepwalker, but I'll kick off
like the Greeks, a naked Athenian actor,
I never wore a prayer shawl.
I read the dictionary of owls,
say Kaddish for myself. Scratch an actor,
beneath you'll find another actor.

I Choose to Write a Poem

I choose to write a poem
when my left ankle's broken, purple,
and my right ankle's swollen blue,
both knees banged, twice their usual size,
both my long legs "killing me,"
while a famous angel is really killing me.
I separate physical pain from the real thing—
the real thing, the soul usually dies
before the body. My soul is dancing,
welcoming spring in the garden
on a beautiful June morning,
ready to live forever.

Water Music

David told me that years ago I said:
"Fishing a Canadian lake is Mozart,
ocean fishing is Wagner." Now I think
in a storm, the Saint Lawrence River
is *Götterdämmerung*, some streams
trill Scarlatti, run into head waters,
where I have fished for Gluck,
Debussy, Stravinsky, Shostakovich.
I caught nothing. I still keep fishing
in musical waters: I caught a perch
in a Chinese Lake that was Puccini,
looked exactly like a perch
from the Ashokan Reservoir.
I trapped crustaceans in the River Thames, Purcell —
his flowing theater and sacred music,
not far from Devil's Acre. A little north,
at Oxfordshire where the Thames (Purcell)
becomes Thomas Tallis, I caught rainbow trout,
Salve Intemerata Sanctus et Benedictus.

* * *

Missa Solemnis from Bach to Weber
is like fishing for a "manager fish"
in the Caribbean, where slaves had to save
the best fish for their manager.
Take the Dead Sea, lowest point on earth,
lowering every year—where there's no music
or fish in the sea's murderous salt,
there are bacteria colonies near shore.
Still a diver in full salty gear told me he's heard
someone or something practicing

bubbling-bassoon-scales at sea bottom,
the "clown of the orchestra," bassoon.
The Dead Sea Scrolls may be read
basso profondo, or by castrati
in their lost art. Since we first became human,
when we fished, and hunted, there was music,
love songs much like a leopard's purring,
hands clapped to dance, heel and toe percussions;
mamas hummed wordless music that became lullabies.
Visiting fisherman, I quickstepped barefoot
over sharp Dead Sea stones to swim,
Goddamn, I cut my feet, but
the tough bare-footed Israeli I swam with
stepped and danced on the stones
as if he were in a make believe ballroom.
I asked him with a smile,
"Do you think your feet might not be Jewish—"
a poet soldier, he didn't like my joke.

* * *

I remember how friends swim,
and those who cannot swim,
original and conventional swimmers.
They carried invisible musical instruments.
No beach umbrellas. I netted crawdads
near New Orleans, where the Mississippi
became Bunk Johnson, Louis Nelson Delisle,
Louis Armstrong, Sidney Bechet, the Hot 8,
depending on Ole Miss's mood.

* * *

Traveller, not Robert E. Lee's horse,
I was an underwater swimmer in Copland's Hudson
without sheet music, mask, or snorkel.
I would go down 30 feet, hear the music
of cold water in my ears. Was it Bernstein's *Candide*?
Music is not about anything, just notes.
I heard cadenzas, never a full orchestra.
I dived with my dog Sancho after rocks
into a brook, the Bushkill, John Cage—
a dog-man game we both loved.
If Sancho was hunting in the woods,
I didn't have to whistle to call him,
I played opera on a phonograph and he'd come
swimming across the John Cage Bushkill
from the often twelve-toned wilderness
of Schönberg, where Arnold was
the Rondout Reservoir, full of *Sprech Musik*,
between singing and speaking,
a *Pierrot Lunaire* waterfall. Sancho would run
through water music in the Dorian mode,
somewhere between universal Stravinsky's
The Rite of Spring and Debussy's *Sunken
Cathedral*— depending on the season. From a glen,
I saw Satie trickle, refusing to be grand.
I heard Berg and Bartók were flooding in Vienna.
Beauty, I bet my life, is not an entertainment,
it ennobles—contrast, not conflict,
F means *forte*, "loud," not war. Yes, there is
reiteration, overtones, dissonance, harmony
vs counterpoint. Two melodic lines may go together.

Still there are those who prefer a person's body
on many occasions to his or her art.

31

I'm Sorry

—To W.H. Auden

I'm sorry, exhausted, except for funds.
I wrote a check, the date October 18
without the year, to Theresa Monrose
for a hundred dollars, I did not write
the amount longhand.
My conversation with friends
is something like the way I wrote that check
when I try to tell what I owe them.
I don't get it right, I leave off years,
the everyday debt made clear by saying
something like thank you,
in a handwritten letter.
Yes, I believe everyone's
time of day or night is different.
I'm sure a poet I love,
who demanded punctuality,
never bounced a check.
When he died, age 66,
at the Altenburgerhof Hotel,
he did not pay his bill.
I guarantee the world will pay
for his empty *zimmer* a hundred years.
I can't get Siegfried's Funeral March out of my ears.

Mishearing

I said they concluded letters with
"Yours in the <u>bowels</u> of Jesus."
Neilson heard "balls." An egregious
mishearing, best forgotten.
To age is not to rotten.
It does not often happen,
a child with no father or mother
is an orphan,
a confusion of "oftens"
never happens.
Brothers, I look for a religion,
I fight a revolution
to make laughter a form of absolution.
There's a good and evil laugh.
A laugh cut in half
is not a smile. A hangman's rope
cut in two is not a string.
A telescope may show spring coming
in winter. A sinner and the Pope wait
for a Second Coming.
I've never touched holy water,
but I've bathed in beautiful oceans and lakes.
I could write a book of my mistakes,
illegitimate son and daughter—
there are no human fakes. Mannequins are fakes.
Lies are lies, not fake words.
If I could, I'd kiss words and birds.
I'd kiss the impossible
and the Bible. Infallible,
the Pope speaks *Ex Cathedra*. There's the rub,
Pope Francis leaves a ring
of ashes and dust in his bathtub.

I would wash his feet and that ring.
I would not kiss the ring on his finger.
A villanelle may be a dirge.
What news on the Brooklyn Bridge,
Roses are often Jews.
Forget-me-nots are not Huguenots.
A cross is not two sticks.
A religion sticks for life, especially if you're Catholic.
My heart cheers for the Beatitudes and Psalms,
sometimes I write fire alarms.

Frivolity

The differences between wind and spirit
are material; their similarities
cause confusion among the trees
and holy doves. You see wind moving, hear it,
see what it does to water. No doubt
it filled sails, moved humanity round
the world. Still, wind and spirit I found out
are the same word in Hebrew.
After Babel came Hebrew,
then spirit was not the same—
it was Christian, happy with a Greek name.
Houses of worship left unattended,
the north wind, Boreas, a deity
flew Oreithyia to his mortal bed.

Venus was born out of a scallop shell.
I was born with fortunate credentials
in New York City.
My heart beats with frivolity,
it plays with spirit and wind. A pity
on dark 15th Street I heard
a beggar say, "Soon I'll break bread
with the dead."
A gift of the absurd:
I gave him change, a smile, public charity,
not an embrace, a pet.
I write breakfast recipes for fun, this omelet,
something like a prayer without a minion—
take two eggs, Adam, half an apple, a pinch of sin,
grated words and cheese, purple onion,
a pillar of salt, throw Song of Songs in,
Not exactly a revelation,

I sing jingles. It became clear to me since the Creation
that the world is God's opera house,
we are here for His entertainment.
He loves differences: the rat and the mouse,
the raven and the crow, the flea and the louse,
the earth and the world,
the kinky and the curled,
Christmas, nativity, and advent.

In the beginning was the Word not said.
Words were spoken and heard, not read.
In the end, a certain contentment,
a smoothing out, a level
without angels or the devil,
without ascent or descent.
Frivolity is a jig, a poem, a dance,
sometimes a last chance.

Pub Crawl

I have verse on hand, an envelope
addressed "nowness and permanence,"
stamped "please forward."
I've seen charts of the Calpurnian universe,
superseded by the Ptolemaic.
Scientists are judged by their peers, not the public.
"Public" is a word I pull apart with readers
who are raptors, coyotes, hyenas
who stretch and swallow the word "public."
Then came a pub crawl, republic, publicity that
Helen of Troy did not require.
Half deaf, I just heard the syllable choir.
I sing in a choir, I know Hallelujah Choruses
that have nowness and permanence.
I'm running out of ink, I can't develop metaphors.
What can I do with half notes?
Every half note deserves a tune, a life.
Every sound has meaning, is a complicated song.
Living things sing or hum—some are night singers.
Today, I worship sunlight, Aurora, the goddess of dawn.
I don't want to let the morning go, every day is a miracle.

As a child, after a miracle, I addressed the people of the world.
I declared If you can't swim, don't go swimming every day as I do
among the lily pads, frogs and clocks, clocks, clocks,
LIARS.
At best, water clocks tell fables about time,
children's stories. Numbers are fables,
laughter and tears are never counted.

I bow with others before a closed curtain,
we play to an empty house.
I keep a jar of nowness handy,
I think, I sing all of a sudden.
My mouth is a necessity,
my limbs are tools, conveniences,
they hold, embrace, caress,
which my mouth can also do.
Differences are part of each body and soul,
then there is a person, a collection of differences.
I've seen Mister, Mademoiselle, Madam,
differences walking, waiting to cross the street.
I've seen and been part of an audience of differences.
Who am I, who are they?

Differences contend for a silver cup and for life.
Yes, I'd rather be a winner than a loser,
Yes, there's a question each of us must answer:
How will we wave goodbye?
Every open hand, every dead hand
tightens to a fist. My view of the world
on March 10, 2019, right now is that dates lie.
The past is prose, eventually verbs take over.
Date trees can live for centuries.
I used to eat dried dates I now find inedible.
Now I live in a temperate zone
 700 miles from the nearest date tree.
Sooner or later, I'll be a blind date.
Whoever he or she is will likely find me
permanently amusing.
I used to follow the fights on radio and tv,
now the only fight I want to see is Apollo and Herakles
battling for the Delphic tripod.
I've given you an inch of the day left to me.

A March 3, 2020 Birthday Card, Mailed
September 1, 2019 to Michael Schmidt

Michael, very close friend, thank God
you were born to dream in Mexican
and English. ¡Feliz Cumpleaños!
Happy Birthday! Which will bring more happiness?
Opposing armies mobilize
in the plazas and squares, ready to fight
a Thirty Years' War over the writing
on a birthday cake.

Your heart is a subject and citizen of poetry
and prose—you hear Mexico, England,
and stateless singing. Think
of a wilderness of monkeys.
Your heart and my heart are pieces of cake
on two plates. Who can tell the difference?
I do not want guests to do
what Trelawney did to Shelley's dead heart—
cut it out of his all-too-romantic body,
wrap it like a sestina in a silk shroud.
Then, like a sovereign, king and coin,
it was passed from hand to hand
until it tinkled into a counterfeit coffin.
Chopin's frightened sister smuggled his heart
back to Poland pickled in a jar.

I remember when I moved to Barcelona
in 1953, just after
my Tangiers wedding to a Catalan lady.
My father wrote a letter that read, "You have
betrayed your country." I destroyed
the letter, thinking I should hide it

from God's eyes. A few of my friends say,
in a chorus, "I told you the son-of-a-bitch
believes in God."

I stray, you do not. I repeat myself.
Rather than simply saying "I love you,"
I stroll across a battlefield drinking margaritas.
I'm Stanley Belch—red, white, and blue garters
betimes Falstaff's Swallow.
You've lived an impossible life, therefore
your poetry is impossibly beautiful,
your book is full of syllables and beats,
the egotistical sublime of Keats, yourself.
I read your poem out loud about driving
a car that reminds me of Homer,
"swerving claxons," Achilles dragging
Hector's body around Troy,
St. Christopher hanging over the speedometer,
Humanity drags around and around
Eros in Piccadilly Circus.

Why don't we have a birthday breakfast
March 3, 2030, I'll bring the cake.
When will we wish to die, perhaps
when all those we love are dead. In ten years,
we may not choose to find new friends.
Happy Birthday! Feliz Cumpleaños!

Stanley

Random

The General, who wanted to drop 30 atom bombs
on China, addressed both Houses of Congress,
concluded with,
"Old soldiers never die, they just fade away."
He did not say, "The matrix of the everlasting
remains a triangle. *I'll give you what for*
usually means a beating." I want to understand
random matrices and their applications.
What do I overstand? Of course I grandstand
take my stand, I play a panpipe on a bandstand.
In London, I walk along the Strand toward theaters,
stepping carefully over the homeless
sleeping on Underground grills.
I bone myself, my grilled sole at the Savoy.

A random triangle of numbers,
equilateral numbers not likely. History weeps
like a baby in the ruins of Nanking in 1937,
an unknown number of years after Big Bang.
Is it a fact nothing is random, meaningless?
I search for a meaningless word—
stupid, no word is meaningless.
I look for a meaningless full stop past the stars
in the night sky, I sometimes make out Venus.
Without words, punctuation becomes pop art,
red question marks, black commas.
Take the sexual commingling of all living things,
note the triangles in full light and darkness,
the angles, the mob, the overpopulation.

Still Trafalgar Square is almost a hexagon.
I do not count the steps of the winding stair

that leads to the National Gallery—
given the overpopulation, I have no doubt
someone fell down those steps to his or her death.
I attend services at Saint Martin in the Fields,
I drop into a pub for a beer and pie,
I drink till closing time. With a clay pipe,
I blow soap bubbles, *X X X*.
I blow Churchillian cigar smoke at the universe,
my contribution to the arts and sciences.

Thou shalt not go from concentration camp to a slumlord.
Still it is a given for most they should,
 "Do unto others as you would have others do."
In every bed a triangle, the family romance, odd numbers.
I was told as a child to keep my hands under the table.
Today I have my left swollen foot on the table,
proof, if you want proof, of the everlasting.
"…Words without thoughts never to heaven go."

They Plow Their Father's Field

I taught English poetry in Beijing
30 years ago. I thought
there has to be a special name
for Chinese work,
working the same field
in the same way with the same
wooden implement, the plow
looked Chinese 8000 years ago.

The shape of a character in calligraphy
is not work or labor or farming or plowing—
is part study, part poetry.
The character for truth is a real theory.
For the name of the girl,
the dead poet's daughter,
the character is plain
but the meaning is Extraordinary.
Her brother is Sho-fan, Sunshine,
he is a poet
works for Tel and Tel.
Both children are often lonely.
Their surname Yang means Flute.
They are their mother's joy,
they plow their father's field.

—To He Huaren

Zigong, Salt City of China

In Zigong, salt city of China,
the spring rain suddenly stopped.
On the first summer day sunlight went deep
into the ravines. In the cold climate,
I chose to walk in an unfamiliar garden.
There were peach blossoms to the west
and plum blossoms toward the east wall.
Although I walked alone, I said "Beauty, beauty."
I did not say peach blossoms were not as white
as plum blossoms. The peach blossoms fell into a rage,
flaming red to the very roots of their hair,
their faces redder and redder with accusation.
But I intended no harm, no offense.
There was no reason for anger.
Pity me on my birthday, the first day of summer,
when flowers have their ways completely beyond me.

China Poem

In China, the people give importance
to what they call "spring couplets," paper sayings
pasted with wheat-flour and water
above and down the sides of doorways
ancient and just built.
On the entrance to a cave house,
I saw, right side, on red paper, in calligraphy:
"Strive to Build Socialist Spiritual Civilization."
On the left, on pink paper:
"Intellectuals: Cleaning Shithouses for Ten Years
in the Cultural Revolution Clears the Head."
Across the lintel:
"When Spring Comes Back, the Earth is Green."
The Chinese know they enter and depart
through the doors of poetry. I was on my way
to the Great Wall that can be seen from outer space.
Wondering, I stopped at a rural place.
Stranger, I was greeted lovingly
by an old mother. I was offered tea,
welcomed into her one room stone house.
There was a framed photograph
of a young man on a table, some books,
a red brick stove bed for a family.
I told He Huaren, a dead poet's wife,
"In that room, I saw a great civilization."
On our way, we passed a cemetery.
Two women and a man
kneeled at the grave of a dead ancestor,
touched their heads to the ground.
Then, standing up, they burned paper money.
From the distance, I saw fireworks lighting
half the sky in the afternoon thirty years ago.

II

Stage Left, Stage Right

Squall

I have not used my darkness well,
nor the Baroque arm that hangs from my shoulder,
nor the Baroque arms of my chair.
The rain moves out in a dark schedule.
Let the wind marry. I know the Creation
continues through love. The rain's a wife.
I can not sleep or lie awake. Looking
at the dead I turn back, fling
my hat into their grandstands for relief.
How goes a life? Something like the ocean
building dead coral.

    —SM

Joy

Death wears a gaudy fig leaf,
gaudy, from the Latin *gaudium*, joy.
I am taken back. I cheer for *Nothing*,
Elizabethan slang for female genitalia.
I know, *Something* doesn't mean penis.
In the wilderness there's a deflowering,
still wildflower *Somethings* enter *Nothings*.
A mirror shows me sporting,
gauding with my familiars,
an engagement, not a marriage of life and death.

A loudspeaker told the crowd,
"An honor to his race, Joe Louis."
Prizefighter, African American,
lost his first fight to Max Schmelling,
who wore a gaudy swastika in 1936.
In 12 rounds he knocked out Louis,
to the joy of the German-American Bund
and America-Firsters.
Second fight, Louis knocked out Schmelling
in two minutes the first round,
Chamberlain prime minister.
Fritz Kuhn, leader of the Bund,
Lindbergh, and half of America wept.
I cheered, got a kick in the ass
from Johnny, my nanny's German boyfriend.
For me and many others for many gaudy years
it was Washington, Lincoln and Joe Louis.
Later I found out Schmelling was celebrated
in Israel. He was anti-Nazi.

* * *

Every living thing is partly every other living thing.
We are forests, one school, one flock, despite our callings,
languages, buzzing, petals flowering,
apples, different wheat, weeds, they all are us.
A few of us are born, then devoured
before we've had a chance to sleep,
The earthworm awakes under the grass,
no other worms kiss it "Good wriggling,
good morning and good night."
How long will I wriggle? How long
will I dance? In the Roseland Ballroom
I didn't trot. "Whites only."

Death is life hereafter,
but what is after that evening?
In slang *Nothing* I will sleep,
far from nada   niente   rien   nichts.

Easy Does It

"Nature never rhymes her children,"
    —Ralph Waldo Emerson

1.

It's easier for me to write a poem that rhymes
than free verse: I keep up with hard times.
Forty percent of our population
thinks the wrong side won the Civil War,
it's 5000 years since the creation.
That was the age of my grandma's samovar—
she used to dance and sing lullabies.
After her son died,
she never let me see tears in her eyes.
Meter and rhyme push my pen a little ahead.
It's fun to conclude I'll live longer than I'll be dead,
I'll move Hollywood to Birnam Wood.
My pen changes me, isn't much good
at changing the world. I'm not Dr. King or Constantine.
I hear the Gospel on a mobile phone,
the Hebrew Bible is a landline.
I do not prefer doorbells to church bells.
These days angels prefer the saxophone
to the harp. Paradise has attics
full of nameless resurrected flesh and bone.
The language of nature is mathematics.
God is not number one.
The telephone rings when day is done—
sorry, wrong number. Like Quixote I eat lentils.
I prefer upright consonants to vowels, faithfully
yours to yours in Jesus' bowels.
Rhyme's not useful as a metaphor, a wheel, or plow.
In our cave dwelling age of artificial intelligence,

past, present, the future soon won't make sense.
How much rhyme can an honest man steal or borrow?
Music may be <u>said</u> in odd,
and even numbers. God is odd
and even. Now Chinese has no future tense.
A language may die like a river,
still the tragic river *King Lear* will flow
with "never, never, never, never, never."
When dove may no longer rhyme with love,
when the four seasons are buried below
the horizon. What reason is there for snow,
when the unbelievable has taken over,
the dictionary drowned, personal pronouns over,
when we are all "its," life is over.

2.

Take it easy, it takes time to go down under.
Most living things have thoughts, I wonder
without a compass except failure.
Naked, all my clothing is unnecessary regalia.
What is the meaning of rhymes?
I do not rhyme for hire.
Desire surrounded, surrenders to desire.
Crossing the ridges of allegories and metaphor,
I look for something timeless, without after or before.
I want to rhyme readers out of their belief
in the lying impossibilities of grief.
Life doesn't end it discontinues.
Take it easy, I believe in the sublime.
I also have the right to sing the blues.
Ancient Latins and Greeks never rhyme
except Aristophanes, who according to Plato knew
their city best. He rhymed to amuse.
Laughter made Athenians think,

stars, clouds, frogs, and giraffes wink.
Wink means *perhaps*. Beware of the certain.
Athenian theater was without a curtain.
To be alive or dead has its place.
Never to be born is a disgrace.

Wishing

I am prey and predator,
all the world is food for thought.
Take the average number of predators,
some starving because of overpopulation.
Life's a battle, lunch on this: Finance and murder cause
disappearing species, no ice age lately.
Prey flies, swims, runs away, hides under,
behind, high in trees, between rock crannies.
I wish to learn at least how much food mostly
human populations need to flourish
or simply survive. I am wary of my verse
that first takes on household obligations,
then the Furies. I write
The helpless calendar of lunar years is prey,
time, the wide winged predator.

In multicolored wounds, there's beauty.
Fuck time heals all wounds.
Thousands of predators swallow beauty.
Kafka speaking for his time, wrote one day:
I can't finish anything. I am afraid of the truth.

Men, women, children have the gift to wish,
we do not simply want, desire, yearn
like all the other living things that cannot wish.
I exercise my right to wish, I say with pen and ink:
few lives and deaths are beautiful as a lion
stepping ever so softly,
then leaping after a gazelle,
like a novelist reshaping life.

My idle reader says, *There you go again*
talking about yourself as if you were me.

You who are neither prey nor predator,
ask the Visigoths, *What became of the eggs*
in the nests of Europe, the platypus and echidna?
They are the only mammals that lay eggs.
Predator, steal an egg, kidnap a child.
Camerado, make it on bread, loneliness,
beans, rice, the staffs of life.
A contradiction, given overpopulation
loneliness will be the last to go.

2.

My closest relative, the chimpanzee, makes it on fruit,
seeds, termites, devoured monkey meat.
I am not surprised to learn sometimes animals
communicate by scratching signals.
I explore my body like a monkey fleas,
just as Lewis and Clark did the northwest—
I pick out rivers, mountains, the great divide.

Gorillas can't swim. There are different populations
on the north and south side of the wide Congo.
South side female leaders in disagreement and conflict
decide by making all kinds of love, not war.
On the north side, male gorillas have dominion,
make war, are cruel to their females
like no other animal but humans.
Nothing lives in the mad water cataracts
and mountains of the Congo—its gigantic
waterfall-Furies misnamed by another Stanley
Livingstone Falls. In the several mile deep
holy river's darkest night waters,

what does the blind Congo eel find to eat?
Then there are those fish who dine
with a mouthful of God knows what in almost boiling water.

I deal in the not impossible.
A worm wants to fly, to make its way through the clouds.
Among packs and herds, there are those
that want to crawl into the earth,
to rid themselves of the predator Day
and the prey called Night. To wish is lyrical,
I wish to be me, I am wild prey and predator,
I do not wish to be something like the ruffled grouse,
prey of a great horned owl.
Born by accident, I consider I'll be reborn
a Baltimore aureole, a flycatcher,
a warbling vireo (Ted Roethke's belovéd bird).
I see I've lost the rights of free speech—
I only speak in parables.
Hillel said, "The more flesh, the more worms."

O Beautiful O Beautiful Girl

A free Phoenician woman gave Sappho
the gift of a necklace, the alphabet,
letter by letter, gold and silver— pearls gathered
from a reef once known as the mother of laughter,
a speck on the wine-dark Oceanus.

Naked except for the necklace, Sappho made love,
wrote letter by letter with her Greek tongue.
In a manner of speaking, she sailed
the known and unknown rivers of Greek
like a woman's body, breasts, and between the thighs
and every port of call. Sappho gave thanks,
consumed by agony, unable to reach
the woman she loved, she suffered *Seizures*.
Afroditi answered prayer, Sappho's heart
filled with fire—the knots of agony loosened,
the goddess almost a shield in battle.
Artemis, the virgin goddess, kept
her distance, Eros never far off.

Spartans thought but for the Phoenician woman's necklace,
the wrath of Achilles would be forgotten,
the teaching of Hesiod lost in seas rolling
with rumor— Greek memory a broken *amphora*,
flooding fields and orchards with wine, trees drunk.
Never! Athens and Lesbos are not fishing villages.
Different pipes and lyres, different music,
the same language in the street and on Parnassus,
Greek is still Greek.
The Delphic oracle speaks, does not write.

The snake of too many questions strikes:
Perhaps the necklace was pinched by Socrates'
wise early grandfather, or exchanged
for a chariot with four horses,
or the necklace alphabet was given
to a beautiful early grandmother of Sappho,
thanks to her passionate favors?

Even these days, in a temple on Lesbos
during a sacred interval, before gifts
are placed at the feet of Athena,
the truth of alphabets is a matter of argument.
Poetry, not love of wisdom nor natural
philosophy, made Greek a sacred language
surrounded by barbaric tongues, the truth
known to every poet worth a grape.

Second Look

Auden sang a lot. I never heard him sing
hymns or Wagner. He liked
Frank Loesser's *Guys and Dolls*. I bet he sang
"If they asked me, I could write a book."
It would be cozy listening to his baritone
"Trust Thou in the Lord," then his *Tristan*.
I guess, older, his voice cracked like his face
from booze, smoke, and love, not 66 years.
It's a little messy to say, "He made me better."
He boned my filet of sole.
He was a blood bank many a time
when I lay in the gutter bleeding.
In Rome, we went to the opera
in 1948,
by truck to the Terme di Caracalla.
Afterwards
I might have said, "Let's sing a duet—
I'll be Leperello, you're the Don."
He might have agreed to be La Statua,
demanding "*Pentiti! Pentiti!*"
I don't know the exact time he demanded.
Do I spend more time thinking of what has passed
or what's to be? I can hear him say,
"Stanley, what about the right now!
You're not a calf, I'm not a cow."

It's My Turn

Once I thought within my compass were the streets,
ways, and sidewalks of an alphabet of cities,
just the Bs, Barcelona, Boston, and Beijing.

Today, early morning I wrote four lines,
Then on Route 9G I drove my Odyssey to Rhinebeck,
the closest town for a good hearty breakfast.
Cousins followed in two cars, headlights on.
A road I had driven hundreds of times,
I made a left turn instead of a right.
It took ten madhouse minutes
before I knew I'd made the wrong turn,
my dear cousins following behind me,
although they knew I was wrong. The ladies
had some gas station deli refreshments.

I write this, questioning my wrong ways,
and why on my return, fifteen minutes
after I got home I tore my right leg
on a nightstand. Bleeding, I write this.
This scene is a comical tragical play,
a comedy of errors:
The Importance of Being Inconsequential.
I was happy to invite my cousins to breakfast.
They drove from Maine to celebrate
my 93rd birthday party for reasons of affection,
and some curiosity.
What might I tell them of family history?
Perhaps my left turn was a way to go back
and redo the past.

Maybe driving two hours after I woke
I kept dreaming a dream I don't remember.
For good luck, I'm telling you how I spent
the morning after my 93rd birthday.
After an hour I returned home to read
Poets at Work, St. Theresa, Hildegard of Bingen.
Did God make me turn left as a gift?
Caution, independent Stanley. You are inclined
to think you are right. How little you understand.
With just a turn of the wrist, you can make
everything wrong from horizon to horizon.

I hold my foot high on a pillow.
No question if I walk across the room,
my swollen leg will start bleeding again.
I've not seen my blood except in a syringe
for years. It's red for danger.
Poetry is dangerous work. One foot on the brake,
at the same time a foot on the gas,
I make a sharp right turn through a STOP sign.
I love red. I have a red mailbox,
a cottage in Canada with a red steel roof.
The world is round, so making a left turn just means
I'll get to Pete's in Rhinebeck late for breakfast.
I can distinguish different breakfasts
in Barcelona, Boston and Beijing.
I'd rather breakfast on *ensaimadas*,
café con leche at the Hotel Colon
facing the cathedral and Gothic Quarter,
in Barcelona, *ciudad de mis amores*,
than on Market Street, Rhinebeck, New York.
I turned left for love of breakfasts I had,
with Eros in the kitchen, making me a *café
latte doppio* in Rome, in Provence a *café rosé*.

Spit Tune

1.

Rodin often spit in his clay. Rembrandt
loaded a brush with feces.
I spit on my mop, my pen that cleans up,
crosses out what I write
on the floor of my notebook, lines like
"bloody American arithmetic,
addition, and subtraction
the language of nature is mathematics."
How many blacks were lynched —
men, women, kids hung.
The men died with hard-ons, semen and blood
on the roots of innocent trees,
branches left for Catholic, Jew, Chinese—
their lynched flesh ironed, mailed as postcards.
Mobs linger, more popular than love,
"hate your neighbor, hate the stranger,
for Christ's sake, jail the coloreds,
win the Civil War."

2.

Every living thing is born good,
even bacteria. The Good spits and shits. Ticklish reader,
the Gods that bless tickle me to death.
Arrogant fool, I want to write an elegy
for every living thing. I can't swing it.
Time is Death's altar boy.
If that boy wants, he can drown us in the desert.
Death is God's manservant. In my house,
time wears out like socks, I believe holes
can be darned by work and love's needles.
But time's loose threads braid into a noose.

3.

Tolstoy wrote "The Death of Ivan Ilyich"
to study Death. Ilyich's beloved servant
raised on his shoulders his master's legs,
washed away his excrement.
Tolstoy—pacifist, vegetarian, enemy
of private property, died at a railroad station,
I spit on Death's infallibility.

4.

I spit into this spit tune: words, phlegm,
and whatever else comes up. Don't laugh,
more than once I threw up ten years.
Every living thing doesn't deserve a song,
a saying, or even a figure of speech.
When there's nothing to sing about,
I am content with remembering,
I share my life's stories in prose baritone.
I've shared my bedroom most of my life
with winged, four-footed, two-footed creatures.
Easy to trap but difficult to hand-wrestle mice,
so if I must choose from among the free-for-alls,
I'll choose the singular. There were times I got it right —
and poems I never wrote that I might have written,
unremembered. In metros, subways of the mind,
words my tickets, I passed through turnstiles, dreams.
The rub is I may end up just down the street
or elsewhere among the untouchables,
the linguistic disobedients.
I'm certain the always shining sun
will shine for me tomorrow
a good place to end without my usual full stop

For W.S. Merwin

Today is the first day of spring.
In Greek and Hebrew, breath and soul are the same word.
You're dead six days, your breath and soul
banished from the society of your body. Your soul
happy miracle, galloped to Paula, who is Paradise.
She holds you as Mary held Jesus after death
and you hold her in your arms— two pietas.
What are you, where are you
What's your address, arrondissement, zip code
If life's a dream as you told me,
I hope your idea of death is right,
you're both wide awake now,
you still kiss good morning and goodnight.

I hold if you want to understand someone's heart,
find out what breaks it.
I'm dreaming, wide awake: close to the truth.
I'm in the stocks now like King Lear's messenger
because I announced your coming
with a hundred poet-knights who love you.
I also have the right to ask: how many American poets
are Cordelia living in France, destined
to be carried dead in your arms?

Hallelujah! If it were not for Satan
there would be no knowledge on earth.
From now on I'm your seeing eye dog,
a mutt waiting your whistle for me to come.
You will not whistle.
Julian, Gregorian, lunar calendars make you laugh.
Since your death a thousand wildflower,
violet, and trillium years have passed.

I saw a deer and fawn yesterday, both had your eyes.
For all I know, if life's a dream
death's a library, there are afterlife seasons,
books of poetry written by the dead.
Fuck ashes and dust. A wild guess, you bathe
in the surf, in canticle-deep sand,
write poems with your bare feet in sand.
I think you wrote part of this.
If this reaches you, I bet you'd shake your head no, no,
smile, and say, "Not on your life!"
You don't need or want it, but
these words are meant to keep you alive.
My apologies.

Have a Heart, Brain, Kidney, and Lung

I accept that I am an alphabet
without umlauts, accent graves, or cedillas.
True, my letter Os are coming loose,
but I've got three cross-letter Ts.
My ABCs are sleeping.
I take my temperature orally and under-arm,
by the number of songs I sing.
I am available, which is different from able,
one has to be natural to make sense.
Is the word three a better word than we?
I think as I grow older, verbs are my walking sticks,
still I walk with bare feet—
I have split personalities, split again.
When I count the hours on fingers and toes
I never get past twenty—8 o'clock.

Today my apposite diagnosis:
"Age adjusted exemplary shape."
I asked Dr. Franklin, without whose care
I could have been dead long, long ago,
"How long have I got?"
He said, "five years," which is reason for pleasure,
but not for a fool, a shipwreck, a planet like me.
A planet thinks he will never fall from the sky
I accept I will die from planetisis,
but Isis was the Egyptian god of resurrection.
In flight from Sodom, my mother's a pillar of salt,
I am Lot's son left with his sisters. Their thighs
wet with languages and populations.

Happy Birthday Letter to Rebecca Berlow

My advocate, my executor, dear friend,
Auden wrote about love like law
our seldom keeping, often weeping,
nothing about practicing law with love,
that statutory instrument, nothing
like a guitar or sax, more like an organ
at Riverside Church or Radio City.
I suggest with Columbia faculty approval,
you practice law like a Bernini fountain.
Beautiful, not mystical, before the bar
you took the Hippocratic oath,
you swore to your father and mother,
not to Apollo but to Eros on the Torah:
make the world a better place, love,
help the crippled, the sick, the poor.
I'll live a little better because you taught me
wind and spirit are the same word in Hebrew and Greek.
Perhaps on some distant star beyond our universe
life and death are the same word,
flower and lover, law and love the same words.
You teach forgiveness. You hope to teach me
to forgive my son I won't forgive. I am a poor student.
I did teach Margie, when she tried to kill Honey,
"It's better to be a good dog than a bad dog."

I want to teach myself the simple lesson
that it's better to give a sonnet than this.
So what. I'm happy that "this" rhymes with "kiss."
To love is to teach love, not in a classroom
or bed but wherever you are. I try to teach
a maple tree to love me as much as I love the tree,
but it stands there offering shade and wonder,

67

it wants another tree. To learn to speak tree
is harder than Chinese. I wish all your family,
Andrzej, Tessa, your mother, sister, brothers,
and your father a happy birthday.
Because of you, everyone you love is born again.
I'm getting closer to something worthwhile.
My birthday is June twenty-first.
It now is August fourteenth. I'm just sixty
and two days. To wish and believe your wish
is a crescent moon over a Long Island potato field.
Wherever Rebecca sits, she declares love *ex Cathedra,*

a little white smoke comes out of my pen.
I dance the hora, the waltz, the tango and Irish jig,
white Polish and Venetian nights.
I toast in Hebrew I can't write.
To life, especially to you. Happy birthday!
!!!!!! Exclamation marks, not candles.

According to Rebecca and precedence, law is love.
Law must have its preoccupations, worry,
Justice worries, worry is not just concern.
Whatever you do about injustices, you obey law
and love. To love is an infinitive,
love's a noun, mostly a verb.
The truth is decided by a hung jury,
I did not think I would celebrate
your birthday worrying. You put the worry
of every member of your family in a trunk,
I took it home. I opened the heavy trunk,
to my surprise worry was a cage full of birds,
raptors and songbirds flew away. Some worry is stone,
an unmovable rock surrounded by some pebbles.
Human, you drive eighty miles an hour

on a fifty-five mile-an-hour turnpike.
The jury has found you guilty
of love as charged. You are sentenced
to life imprisonment, shackled
to love's ball and chain for life.

Stanley

Xmas Carol

—To Carol Rumens

The homeless celebrate
Christmas in the manger
they do not rest, they wait and wait.
Still, the homeless often love the stranger
although many believe they only have
a home in the grave.
Let's sing a carol.
Stille Nacht or Rumens Carol.
Music says you belong,
dismayed, not long.
There is truth in names and rhyme.
It's not by chance, a trick of time,
that Jesu rhymes with Jew and Hebrew.
The Thou Shalt Nots also tell us what to do.

Snood of Garlic

I took down the broken kitchen clock,
hung a snood of Garlic on its hook.
Ah, if time were only Garlic
lovers might more truly say "My darling,
I'll love you to the end of Garlic."
Years, days, hours, minutes—Garlic.
No longer Happy New Year. Happy Garlic.
Mothers would read to small children:
"Once upon a Garlic." Human beings
being what they are, the Garlic people
fight with the onion people.
I'm thankful for Christmas Garlic, Ramadan Garlic,
and Passover Garlic. How is this Garlic
different from all other Garlic?

Vertigo

I open a book, turn it upside down,
then try to read a page.
The page is the room I'm in
or the street I'm on.
I fall hard and learn
the stone floor is down.
I cover my eyes. It prevents me
a little from seeing and thinking everything
upside down. The world's a merciless-go-round.
Am I having a stroke?
I'm a pocket watch swinging from a tree.

Bedtime Story

I insist my life was, is, an open book
filled with facts no one believes.
Nominative, genitive, accusative stories
about my carnal self. A metaphor:
my arteries carry sentences,
my body, bony, is mostly watery prose
but there is verse in the sound
of my heart's explanations.
Arteries aren't galleries.
My ten fingers and ten toes are proof
my hands and feet run parallel
to iambic pentameters.
I join a mob of bandit faces.
My nose, though Roman, shows less history
than my eyes. No nose ever laughed,
whereas eyes tell the inside story.
My nose may nose around the truth
for the fun of it. I tell you there are
more no's than yeses in Irish beds.
If you follow me, have a double whiskey.
I can find my way home
because I can read glacial scribbling
on granite along the Hudson.
Play with me. I'm more a red balloon
than antique Roman. Full of hot air I let out slowly,
I wheeze the good news.
I'll get to 99 before I'm 100.

I'm disconnected, my lightbulb is loose.
December will end and January will come.
Mercy is the first day of summer.
Bedeviled, when I was thirteen,

I found Rimbaud and Lorca
before I read Whitman and Frost.
I remember in my crib I was given
a green outfielder's mitt. I jumped for joy
I made such a racket I was smacked
down— the first surprise I remember.
Three years old, I heard my father reciting
Shakespeare above my head.
He was studying to be chief of his department
while we walked, he held my hand.
I preferred the gift of *Twelfth Night*
to a green baseball glove.
I don't forget what I cannot recall.

III

Exit

Postamble

Free and equal,
I don't write fiction, a dream book, a novel
with a pen and shovel,
I write a poem about what I do not know
because I want to know.
It's time I let friends and grandchildren know
I stole a branch of laurel from the Delphic Oracle.
I push myself out of my way.
My poem may be something like
a walk in the forest, a serpent's strike,
the 3rd of May, or come what may.
About grammar I've nothing to say,
a shepherd knows
a verb's not a noun in sheep's clothing.
In my soul's playground, today I wrestle
in blue skies with clouds of meaning, loathing
the down to earth. I hear a sparrow's love call
in a noisy city – a sweeter call
deep in the woods, a love call without words.
Lord, I want to understand the languages of birds.

A Lesson

For the known, the very well known
and some I did not know at all,
I rewrote poems, elegy after elegy,
what idle readers didn't need to hear:
briefly we appear, then disappear.
My words gathered in a procession
that stopped, then moved on,
last words for men blessed, a lesson,
women wrapped in prayers and wedding gowns,
some tales running on, a few falling down.
I rewrote poems, stories, some too tall
some comforting, some satisfied my urge
to be comical, tragical, whimsical.

There is no reason to think our Gods have sore throats,
or toothache due to wars or death camps.
Our God abides; ancient Gods took sides.
I wrote nothing providential, my face to the wall.
I looked inside myself. I almost refused to mention
after a death there is no consolation.
We live behind a numbered door, an address.
We die somewhere, north or south,
right here, likely with an open mouth, a deaf ear.

I am contrary.
Sorry, beg pardon, pull out a head of hair.
Death's a holiday, a heavy date, a new year,
with Gregorian and lunar frolicking.
If I have to go, I'll do my croaking
from too much delight, naked, my underwear
swinging from the chandelier,
Eros, crash my funeral! You are

the sweet reason *fun* is a word in *funeral*.
When I'm too tired to take off my clothes or close
my mouth, unlaced, one sneaker on two feet,
may my darling sweeter than sweet-
heart say my name twice. When I'm undone,
I hope I'll think "Thank god I heard her."
My last words, before I'm no one:
"Murder! Murder!"
Unwilling, I'll die ill-mannered, uncouth.
Life's a motherless lullaby, death's the truth.

Ode to Stella Halkyard, Rylands
Librarian Soon to Retire

You have a King's Highway, I've got a turnpike.
Forget Covent Garden, this is Music Hall.
Thank you for giving us Turner-like
beautiful thought, Manchester snowfall
with your views of medieval jeweled Latin binding.
In your care, while you are minding
Persian poetry, treasures of Gothic art
deep in the library you know by heart.
Thank you for saving a button from Whitman's coat,
early Italian studies of anatomy, flesh from Montmartre,
Milton's portrait, what Wilfred Owen wrote.

Since childhood, I thought a library
was a place of worship, that God is books,
that He fishes for us with barbed hooks
and bookworms. To be caught by Him is Merry
Christmas—a Buddhist-Jewish-Muslim-Hindu holiday.
I believe Rylands is a Godly library,
God is plural: He She You and They.
Stella, may He—all of them bless you, darling keeper,
reading you on the Chinese discovery of paper
is a slap in the face of the Grim Reaper.

I don't want this verse to be
a keepsake for strangers and neighbors to see
on a shelf, or kept in a pretty box.
I want this poem to be
a dog with a shepherd and his flocks,
a study in happy and tragic impossibility.
I don't know if you have a cat or dog,
I would like my dog to be a puppy
in your lap, or if you choose, a log

on a fire to keep you warm,
a shield of Achilles to protect you from harm,
not a souvenir, a song you can read and hear.
In cruel months, when you are a lonely soul,
like all of us, hear this hoot from God's owl.

Stella, easy to love stranger,
I put myself in danger:
to me your writing is your face.
Despite a love of life, I see a trace
of shadow, not eye shadow,
I note you never say I—
My new friend, I don't know why.
What will you write now?
There's poetry in your prose
I smell with my American-Roman nose.
Easy to say, "there there, now now."
There are metaphors in the pronoun I.
I may be a flower, a sigh.

Snake in a Basket of Groceries

1.

Today is Flag Day,
I fly the American flag everyday
from my porch rail, not a flagpole.
I've got a fever and misguided swollen feet.
My housekeeper, nurse, friend, Naomi Etienne,
says if I don't stop working,
she'll call the police.

I have no memory of falling asleep,
I only remember waking up.
Mayday, mayday!
I call to myself for rescue.
I find myself longitude 6 feet 2 ½,
latitude belt 40.
I suck on another's milky words,
half asleep, I hope my apparel oft proclaims me,
I'm true to mine own self.

I cannot remember my Social Security
or fax numbers—the beginning of this.
I don't forget my Naval Service Number:
6161612.
With this snake in a basket of groceries,
how can I develop a metaphor?
I remember the poems of others
that keep me alive, and music
that accompanies me, my closest friend.

The years are silent as water lilies,
buggy, turning brown—

holding onto a twig on a sunny day,
a caterpillar eats through to the edge
of a leaf, builds his chrysalis.
After time enough to change, he breaks open,
unfolds a single black wing,
then two yellow and black wings
open into the world.

Someone is answering my phone calls:
"Is anyone there?" *Moshi moshi,*
hello, in Japanese. Hard to believe
no one said "Hello" before the 19th century.

2.
Chief Petty Officer Young told us
the Captain expected 30% casualties.
It didn't turn out that way,
except among my boyhood friends—
the percentage was higher.
I was decorated face and chest
by the red and white ribbons of Jerry's brains.
Arthur lost a leg. Danny the pianist
had his spine made into an accordion.
I'm told at Auschwitz a bowl of soup
shared by four was "paradise."
God had them on a leash,
or was it the other way around.
Truth is not factual,
has pockets, saves words like money,
half truths small change, wherewithal.
A commandment every father older than his sons
hears: *Thou shall send your boys to war.*
You will live longer.

In Tuscany, I visited a villa, ancient vineyards
that were also a cattle and pig farm. The Count complained,
"Germans stole my Renaissance locks and keys."
I was shown 19th Century wine presses,
ladies dancing on Montepulciano grapes,
two dogs "not allowed in the house."
There were stalls where pigs were kept.
I didn't say to my host: *Pigs are highly intelligent,*
clean, sweet as dogs in the house,
they have beautiful memories, grunt appreciation.
It's human pigs that have made swine of them.
To kill a pig is easier than killing a child.
God knows I haven't had a ham and cheese sandwich
for years. I'm a volunteer in two armies:
Salvation and Damnation.

Whimper

My dog Honey suffered two jaw bone operations.
She would not eat, take painkillers
or antibiotics. I found it painful.
She will die. Next day she ate
raw ground beef. I still worried she will die.
Jane said, "We will have her for awhile."
There are different kinds, varieties, of everything.
Naomi and I just lost a significant
part of our lives I may be able
to describe another time.

Elegy for Emily Fragos's Cat Sue

Sue, I wish you came to my farm, a guest,
under or on the dinner table. I'd be proud
to have you. You could sleep on my chest,
your nose in my neck. You and I know that
in Eden, in the tree with the serpent, there was a cat,
your inheritance. Wise games are played by you,
leaping from Emily's love and pillow

to a sonata, Emily playing the cello.
No other feline ever came close to
understanding Emily's poetry.
You heard poems in the works—out loud,
the sound of weeping and laughing constantly.
You never chased a lonely, artless cloud
or meowed off key. There was Emily's whispering

playing a lion or tiger purring
with happiness. Now there is sorrow.
I hope you hear me. Despite a welcome mat,
you're not at the door. I wish you'd ring
a Buddhist doorbell.
Loneliness can fill an apartment.
I am confused. I pour milk in a bowl.
In death's kitchen, what use is a moon or soul,

a cuckoo clock, or Athena's owl?
You thought loving kindness paid the rent.
Now you're behind some gate or stone fence
and I'm speaking to you in the past tense.
At Emily's, you made life merry.
Where your bed stood is a little cemetery.
Now we celebrate Christmas, Thanksgiving,

days of Lent like kittens beyond understanding.
Emily plays the cello, writes poetry for cats' ears.
Your face at the window appears and disappears.
Where you were, the world's a better place,
It seems your eyes were made to see through
Death's curtains, Babylonian lace.
No goodbyes. I want to say hello to you.

Twins

You phoned, a voice I thought, without thinking,
I would never hear again.
We talked about what was left of us.
You asked, "What's new?" I did not say,
"Beyond Einstein, the theory of uncertainty—
time travels in various directions,
gravity pulls time in different directions."

I still believe in the intelligence of clouds.
Feeling and thinking are twins,
they are not identical.
A question, *Who are you?*
will cause different answers.
One twin may answer, "Don't know who I am,"
the other brother or sister replies,
"I feel I'm a stranger."
Anyone can say, "I feel love, I don't think it,"
a wolf howls, "Love has reasons."
One twin says, "I love you, I want to touch you,"
another, "I love you. Touch me."

Twins have the same mother and father.
Poetry and Music are twins—
when they play together, they are songs.
In opera words are often not heard or held too long.
Their games the blues, oratorios,
scat, operas, torch songs.
They wrestle, Music is on top.
Who is the father, who is the mother?
The Greeks thought they knew, they had

a separate part of speech for twins.
After practicing, Itzhak Perlman said,
"A violin is the replica of the soul."
He did not need to say, "The orchestra
is delighted twins can play Bach's Concerto
for Two Violins."

To Alexander Fu Who Wanted to Be a Cosmologist

September 27th and 28th,
two dark rainy days.
Alex was crying for no reason.
He said, "I thought summer was longer.
It's cold. It's already autumn."
Embraced, no one told him
you must learn to love
fall, winter, and spring.

I did not say beware of perfect happiness.
A tree without leaves is full of whispering.
Bats are 1/5th of the world's mammal
population. Viruses are polysexual.
Age 10, he wanted to be a cosmologist.
I write this 7 years later.
Alex looks down, fingering his computer.
He composes music, temperate melodies
made for all seasons.
I have his discarded fiddle
I will paint blue.

Gaudy Ode

God in three persons is gaudy.
Joyful, I love a dove, the holy ghost.
Bread is holy, but not toast.
Some old pretty girls are bawdy.
Red wine may be dry or sweet. Blood is gaudy.

Before Nicaea, pride was not a sin.
The Virgin wore a gaudy dress
soaked with holy blood, a dress
she washed with tears. She hung roses and linen
on a clothesline with praying clothespins.
A heretic clown somersaults
off a Roman cross. He barks at the appalled
crowd, "See the virgin naked all in all.
Drop a coin in the poor box,
then compare Venus's famous locks
with the Virgin's and Magdalene's Jewish hair."
Saint Peter the three-times denier
was told by Jesus the Jew, "On this rock
I will build my church, where
death has no power." The rock is deaf.
Death and life are man and wife.
Who is man, who is wife?
Naked death wears a gaudy fig leaf.
There's death, a bastard twin, in every baby carriage.
Life and death hold hands. God performs the marriage.

Requiem for Ice

40% of Greenland's ice melted in one day.

Pretty old, I choose to misbehave, I curse,
I say there is no winter season anywhere,
the ice on the moon is water,
we will never see a full moon again.
However, Selene the moon goddess
waves a congregation of oceans
to rise, to stand, to fall to their knees.
She is seen at night, still

hearing prayers to the new moon
in the sunflower fields of yesteryear.
The morning sun visits.
I see the shadow of my hand and pen,
a surprise on my lined notebook page
I open my hand and see the shadow
of my fingers moving wherever I wish.
I choose to write. The shadow disappears.

Choirs sing: My Lord, is ice Jew, Catholic
or Protestant water? Enough, enough. Amen.
The Chinese pull the rickshaw of lunar years,
have a museum of modern waters,
afterlife gardens and rice paddies.
Swans walk in pain,
the snow owl cough-hoots in terror,
tries to swim with seagulls.

White rabbits swim with water rats.
Water cities: Amsterdam, Venice, Petrograd

sunk to the ocean floors, are coral reefs.
Now carp and turtles swim through the belfries,
Why do the squid hide in the poor box?
Eskimos who have seven words for snow,
without sleds walk, get lost, need huskies
to smell them back to their melting towns.

Alley cats often leap from tree to tree
like monkeys to avoid water in the streets,
the white tigers of the Himalayas
weep without tears.
If the innocent were slaughtered now,
the flight to Egypt is in a skiff,
the Christ Child swaddled in his lifejacket,
a donkey swimming behind.

There are those who believe there never was ice.
I sing the days of wrath, the second death,
when great drops of ice, every one
according to *Revelation*
came down out of Heaven on men.
David is witness, Earth is ashes.
The Judge comes and demands to know
the strict exact reason for the word *ice*.

Sunny Day

What of the winds' coming and going,
poetry and painting can show winds
moving through this spring's uncut grass,
dandelions down the lawn.
In different countries there are often
different names for the Lord and dandelions:
England's *golden lads, chimney sweepers,*
France's *dent de lion*, Ireland's *Irish daisies.*
Some grasses bend toward a sugar maple,
others bend away on the same hillside
because an oak has partially blocked the wind.
No one can count as many dandelions as I can.
I can write and paint a little.
There are ways of telling in words what is,
while a painter may paint the same thing—
sometimes things equal to the same thing
are not equal to each other.

There are words for colors, and colors for words.
Your sparrow, owl, dandelion is feathered,
petaled for passionate reasons.
I cannot smell a cherished owl or sparrow.
In the wind I smell the flowers nearby.
My faithful senses have intercourse
with every available living thing—
on some summer days, I could shout, "Rape!"

I'd rather have ink dry on the page, rewrite,
rewrite, than wait for oils to dry on canvas
before I change colors, burnt sienna
to cobalt blue to Mediterranean.
I mix powdered pigments for paintings and poems:

a poem's pigment is sound,
the different intimate voice of every word.
In English, there are changing wordcolors,
English is "country dancing" since the Normans—
half truths, how trees spend their weekends,
true to nature, indifferent to seasons.
Music or thunder can be a painter's model.
Beauty does not interrupt me
like a deer or groundhog in the garden.
Lightning catches my eye. Thunder encourages me.
Yes, it is poetry to say
no sunny day is like any other day,
no rose like any other—
there are lookalikes for lazy eyes.
Words use us. On a sunny day,
I try to follow the winds' comings and goings.

Ode to a Snapshot

Today I saw a snapshot of W.S. Graham,
a young man in Scotland or London.
We were friends, almost chums in the Village
in the postwar early 1950's.
I did not recognize Sydney.
His face is completely out of my head.
I don't shave looking in a mirror daily,
I'm not good at recognition.
I repeat this story:
when I woke up at the Hotel Lugano,
I saw an old guy I did not know
in red pajamas in my mirrored room.
When I see photos of my much loved dead
golden retrievers, black labs, and mutts,
I cannot often tell who's who.
Sometimes I know Dulcie, Horatio, Sancho,
Luke, by the age of the trees they stand beside.
My arms are full of dead friends,
wildflowers, annuals, perennials.
My house smells of poets and their books.
Thanks to their poetry, my memory, less faulty
tells lies, faceless lies. That gorgeous girl, 23,
is wearing a mask that says she's 75.
What's her name?

I have more faces than the moon,
I see the moon's half-face above the trees.
There are faces I've known
eye to eye, nose to nose, archived
in files I keep in my donkey barn. I lose names.
It would not be better, it would be medieval
if we were all headless horsemen or

headless horsewomen, searching for our heads.
Now the merry-go-round is going faster, faster,
round and round the world,
the 35mm film reel is going faster, faster,
people are just colors. The movie stops on cue.
There are no photographs of the grand invisible
finale some call sleep, unleavened heaven.

After first light, 67 years obscures a face.
I've never seen a soul fly out of a mouth.
Poor souls are locked behind a fence of teeth,
eventually unlocked when death comes,
not just by good or evil, but by
Shakespeare's beautiful vocabulary,
the uninflected English tongue.

At dinner, Dylan Thomas and Sydney got into a fight,
fought the Scotch and Welsh wars again.
Dylan said, "You should go to intelligence university.
I'd spit in your eye,
but there's so much spit there already it wouldn't fit."

Anything I write has something to do or not do
with the prime protectors of the English language.
In wise and silly ways
meter, accents, and syllables vow to honor languages,
the holy and profane orders and disorders.
Versifiers start and put out fires,
they write in full face, profile,
blinding light on pages,
walls, tablets, parchment, turtle shell.
Much not written at all, simply spoken,
is remembered.

Who Am I to Say?

History is ordinary, but not W.H. Audenary.
It was Audenary to give to the poor.
He wanted to love the stranger.
There is the Episcopal Church's Ordinary.
Ordinary robes: Celtic white, liturgical blue,
multicolored embroidered translators.
On a given day, given everything he wrote,
Caliban's talk before a lowered curtain
gave Auden the most pleasure.
I thought his own soul granted his prayers.
Did he prefer kissing Chester good morning or goodnight?
Did he love Chester more than an infant in the manger?
The question, "Without question
is religion a suggestion?"
I hope I'm right, he believed after the fall
in William James' "concupiscence of evil"
and his God, the All-in-All.
Thank You, Fog crossing the Atlantic
in a pocket will last longer
than a cargo of whisky and Capulets.

These Days

I am diminished.
I think in a new grammatical tense,
the forgotten familiar.
Reading, I still learn what I don't know.
Hard of hearing, I sometimes hear something
beautiful and moving in familiar music
I did not hear before.

If life were tennis, it's match point,
I've lived much longer than I have to live.
Let ball, I'm a better friend now
to friends I still have,
I've lived down my old reputation
backstage that I'm "the tornado."
Not in old obvious ways, I love more. I slice,
I don't sneeze because of feather pillows, cut grass.
Racists and bigots I see as beyond redemption,
although I know that is not quite true.
I ace, foot fault, slam, a forehand winner.

I drink less, because after a few, I sleep.
After three hours at the Prado, I got dizzy
not enough blood in the brain.
I was heading for the Café Murillo
where I sat, had a *bocadillo*, iced tea,
just beyond the statue that thinks "the sleep
of reason produces monsters."
I passed a gifted African painter.
I didn't stop to help him, or commit the sin
St. Theresa warned sisters against, curiosity.
I was sad to lose a possible friend.
There's something wrong in my mind's machinery.

How different are these days from old days.
I prefer "old days" to "the past."
The past, famous for not even being past.
I might list things I can do I didn't do
in the old days, I didn't shoplift poetry,
a few words, images. It's a shame,
writing my old books I did not steal,
except from ancient and gutter languages.

I say things for no apparent reason
out of context more and more often.
I write to discover the reason.
The unknown is good soil,
my wondering becomes reasonable,
a metaphor, seed and plough,
sunlight and rain, verse.
I've come to a page in last year's notebook
in which I should not be writing,
dated June second, 2018—
where despite the fact I was hospitalized,
my left ankle broken purple, my right ankle
swollen blue, I wrote, "My soul is dancing,
welcoming spring in the garden
on a beautiful June morning,
ready to live forever."

I wrap this poem in a misfortune cookie.
I leap, I leap, I leap.
I give this rabbit to a Mongolian falcon.
If I get back to China, I won't walk
the Great Wall as I did from Langzhou,
I would see good friends, I have a Chinese brother—
and possibilities that I have distant relatives
in Lithuania, murdered doornails. I'm
an old dog that smells under the tail of history.

Mothers and fathers of the world, you're like me,
a distant cousin of every living thing.
Around my house there are trees
of various nationalities I love.
I'm proud foxes, squirrels, hummingbirds
and snakes give me their time of day.
I hear populations of tree-dwellers calling,
complaining in languages
I understand better now than in the old days.

A True Berlin Short Story

Christopher Isherwood
said, "a half million homosexuals
were murdered in death camps."
Someone corrected him,
"you're wrong, only 300 thousand."
Christopher answered,
"I'm not in the real estate business."

Low A

Why do I need to mirror
my concave barbershop dentist academic
vulgate general medical practitioner,
my scientist revolutionary inheritance,
my shtetl shoemaker-scholar cousins
murdered in Kovna, circumciséd dog?
I swallowed history, cheese for a rat.
One 5 a.m., sleepless in a king-size bed,
with difficult sadness I found I'd sketched
on the side of a lined page
Auden shaving in two mirrors,
one face young, one face 66,
a wise and loveable wrinkled maze.
His mother taught him on an upright piano.
The lowest note on my piano is a low A—
most old pianos don't have that range.
I do.

50th Anniversary Poem for Cella and Norman Manea

Happy Love may appear and disappear,
contrary to what you seldom hear,
it's easy to share what you love,
a novel, an aria from Rosenkavalier;
a wife and husband can share love
with a cat, a dog, an apple tree outside
their window. Watching lovemaking from above,
the moon between the bedposts. Hatred is worldwide.
For fifty years Cella and Norman's love
has been a gift to the world.
Their marriage made the world
a better place—a Jewish preoccupation.
Somewhat after the Creation,
the Gaon of Vilna pointed out to Kant,
Jews think it's a disgrace, hide their face
if they don't do unto others what they want
others to do unto them. A psalm is not a hymn.
A bookseller and a baker of honeycakes and bread,
among the Maneas' honored dead.
Looking for an honest man, Diogenes had a lamp.
Age 5 in a Transnistrian death camp,
Norman was taught honest murder at that university,
in its secret kindergarten, love and pity.

In Ceausescu's Bucharest, Cella and Norman
were married without a word of Scripture
by Norman's father, an accountant. Alas,
he didn't account to God, who came into the picture
only when Norman's foot broke a glass.
Idle readers, he changed tragedy to levity
and back again, to grateful beautiful gravity.

Norman found that taking off a black hat
was a religious necessity.

Then truth is, he met Cella just in time,
changed their unjust desserts to pantomime.
Those shadows on a sunny day,
never absolutely went away.
While sure as teeth came with biting,
answers and marriage came with writing.
If in the beginning was the Word,
the first word was plural,
light, a cry for help, and a love call.
Puzzled God gave us half-Slavic Romanian,
the bride and groom could not forget the SS, the onion,
the gulag, the Soviet Union.
Fifty years pass. Time needs to unwind the clock,
there's still anti-Semitism right and left.
Proudhon said, "Property is theft,"
Jews are all Shylock.
Cella, a great beauty all her life,
was always a valorous wife— see Proverbs 31.
"She brought him good, not harm, the days of his life."
Sometimes they quarreled for no reason:
yesterday's underwear on the kitchen table,
she cried, "This house is not a stable!"
All for the love of reconciliation.
Of course, Cella won.
There was always Norman and her art,
drawing and restoration,
and thanks to Deuteronomy, well done,
"A circumcision of the foreskin of her heart."

Pocket Mirror

Picasso, age 14, painted a 19th century
sideboard with bottles reflected in a mirror.
Morandi painted bottles without a mirror.
Poets are stimulated by difficulties
inherent in the English language.
There are mirrors behind meaning.
I pity poets who think mirrors are faithful lovers.

After the first word and Light, God created water,
lakes, the first mirrors, the first swimmers.
Near the Yangtze and the Nile,
the Chinese and Egyptian poet-swimmers
saw lovers' faces in copper and silver mirrors,
wrote the Book of Songs, the Book of the Dead.
A wise slave said, "A mirror's the God of deception."

Then Greek mirrors were fashioned into Venetian glass
by natural philosophers.
Thanks to the universal need for mirrors,
Eros was blindfolded. Without reason
I look at your hand and try to see your soul.
Madness to think every part of the body is a mirror.

There are mirrors behind using
commonwealth and foreign prosody,
Irish poetry behind English bottles and glasses.
Slàinte! Lechyd da!* Cheers, mirrors
Harp whiskey and dark ale on Celtic roundtables,
Irish lace tablecloths hung on a wall.
Wearing his red bedroom slippers,

tipsy on English difficulties, lover of God and Miss God,
near home, Auden was comforted by Koine Greek
and Old Church Slavonic liturgies he did not understand.
Rimbaud, Mallarmé, and Baudelaire were behind
young poets who died for France.

*Irish and Welsh toasts

Galileo, Who Recanted, Told Me the Truth

Galileo, who recanted, told me the truth:
The universe existed long before belief
on earth. A fact that is a loveless thought.
Soon grief came with love to earth. What is his?
What's hers, given the many kinds of love:
Merry Christmas and New Year's Eve love,
lovers who can think of nothing else,
every other thing is false.
Lovers' days are never ordinary.
There are lovers who can't betray and lovers who betray.
At the theatre some can't follow the play.
I see from my telescope
a universal dance hall. I turkey trot, I grope
in the fog of my verse for a way,
not Buddha's way, to save my life.
There is yesterday, tomorrow and today.
Whatever fate, how much is love worth?
More than anything, I'll bet my life.
Poetry can die. If I lose I'll bet my life.
I'm using the word *love* too much,
making Apollo and Eros hunchbacks.
In a world without music or holidays
mostly boiling oceans and volcanos
my faults are mine, not Galileo's.
The sun will elope with earth
per second per second—till then love will stay.

Ode to New York City Trees

Our trees separated by cement
seem discontent
they grow fewer
sharing rain with the sewer.
The city, home to raptors and doves
is a lonely forest
my windowsill and fire escape a nest.
There is a treeless subway, sometimes an El
above a crown of trees,
the A train stops, moves
at the mercy
of archaic electricity,
squeaks like poetry in prose.
There's no prose in poetry
or paradise in hell
no hell in heaven.
Music is the only art in heaven.
If you pray on your knees
standing or not at all.
I hope there will be trees
after skyscrapers fall,
become stone and window hills.
Thank God there is a Brooklyn angel,
a bridge that is immortal.

Poem for Naomi

My darling lady from St. Lucia,
Naomi Étienne,
knows the past from future
as if they were gentlemen
who kiss the hand of the present,
ask for a dance, not where the past went.
Does the past hide in a crowded bus?
Naomi kicks the devil under the bus,
praises Jesus.
Time, according to my bad book, is a brood
of vipers versus the will of God.
I put it another way: time is breakfast,
there is a U-turn in the road.
There is some aftertime coming fast—
time was lunch yesterday and supper last night,
time is corn on the cob, we eat from left to right.
Yes, there's still a clock on Babel's tower,
with no hands, no one knows the hour.
Every day I must remember time is food,
a specialty, whatever my mood,
walking up Yeats' winding ancient stair
to receive Judgment's *croix de guerre*.
We must devour death before it eats us.
In the last race everywhere,
Life's the hare, death's the tortoise.
Dear friend, look what you've made me do.
This is my way of saying good morning, love you—
God's honest truth, death's a hare, life a tortoise.
Then there is the chattering, singing rest
of us who know whatever time it is, we're blessed.

I Admire a Brave Ant on my Tablecloth

I admire a brave ant on my tablecloth
taking a breadcrumb to a colony
outside the house, a deaf hero.
A poet who could sleep through bombings,
Enzenberger wrote *Political Crumbs*.
On this Catskill summer evening,
I delight in the proximity of stars
millions of lightyears apart.

Who invented longing and belonging?
I propose we are made for double beds,
each to each and beyond reach.
Dark clouds smother proximity,
the beauty of the world.
A universe far from here resents
our revolving fashions, our values,
the length of a skirt, hat shops

on the Faubourg St Honoré.
Apollinaire thought stars read,
attend black hole collége.
English is such a young language
few stars think it worth learning.
They study distance and gravity,
they live with each other in silence
like practicing Capuchins.

Muslims were first to understand stars.
On the ship of death *S.S. Proximity*,
starboard is left, portside right,

crossing the blind ocean.
When will we drop anchor, tie up?
Astrology, apocrypha! Shining stars
are a form of spelling and misspelling.
I half believe a harlequin

addressed Death's crew
spoke in French (my translation)
dressed in Picasso blue: "*Enfants!*
Moses was given a commandment
shouted in his ear, *Keep proximity*."
Death is ugly, to hold Christ's dying
for all of us is beautiful. I believe
in the nothingness of everything—crumbs

ashes, the date, dust, under a female moon.
I consider notes, words, pigments,
rocks have a certain significance.
Bet your life creation is still in progress.
I read Goethe for beautiful meanings,
seeing one painting, he wrote, changed his life.
What can one person do? Damn proximity,
compose before you decompose,

shout help! help! in the ear of stammering Moses,
make a hero of an ant in a wild rose.

Forest Fires

God did not invent candles or electric light bulbs.
He invented forest fires, the sun, electricity.
He has affection for certain volcanoes.
Does He prefer us to smoke?
Forest fires encourage new growth.
I note there are dark matter halos,
that Comets, planets produce no light
are not luminous. Neutrinos pass through
you and me, everything that is or has been
for fifteen billion years, after the flash.

On earth it's hard to believe God prefers
the middle, moderate, temperate zones.
Hell was made for the Devil and his angels.
The Lord invented water, its names and habitation.
He invented the word and argument,
Auden and fog.
Blasphemy I insist amuses Him.
He allows the spirit of the dead to enter
a living person, take possession thereof.

Prayers in so many languages help Him sleep.
Does He dream? You say "He never sleeps.
how can He sleep, His eye on every sparrow?"
He still provides occasional horseshit,
God's love, for birds of a feather.
He invented grapes not wine, wheat not bread,
blind trees He feeds with sunlight and rain.
He invented crossbreeding and hybrids—the living.
He did not invent metaphors, the psalms,
versification, artificial intelligence.
Milton justified the ways of God to man,

creation vs invention.
I sum up: the Lord created colors not paint.
Paint cracks, falls off walls, mosaics last longer,
gardens survive without any human attention.
He prefers gardens to city streets
with their skyscrapers and glass windows.
His face is everything we see and cannot see—
what? Where?
In our cottage near Chalk River, Ontario,
lightning struck a white pine.
Surrounded by forest fires, I heard
Protestant and Catholic bells
summoning the volunteer fire brigade.
Inside the cottage, a forest fire,
man and woman, tongue, flames
leapt over, and into the skin and hair,
the taste of perfection, going in and out
slowly and quickly, deeper and deeper,
each conquers and surrenders,
smells and tastes everywhere—
each a god and God's messenger.

Perhaps south is His mouth,
everywhere His hair.
Does He need money? Perhaps water is His currency.
Does He prefer to be called Father
or another of His forty-four names?
Dearest forest fire, I cannot say "I Love you,"
sometimes I prefer a pond to ocean,
a lit match to a forest fire,
a rocking chair to an earthquake,
today, an act of a woman to an act of God.

A Smiling Understanding

There is an understanding,
a smiling understanding,
between orchards and orchestras.
Jazz and Bach are fertilizers,
something extra. Trees are much older than music
and poetry, were gods for good reasons.
They have bodies and souls. Trees are choirs,
mezzo sopranos, coloraturas,
tenors and baritones, castrati.
I live with music and trees, orchards of music,
woodwinds and sextets. I sing
the "I don't lie to myself" blues.
I learn from my suffering to understand
the suffering of others. I climb musical scales.
Trees have an embouchure. I'm a sapling.
Breath and wind blow through me.
This winter is a coda of falling leaves,
sequoias and magnolias Louis Armstrong
Coltrane willows, citrus, and evergreens.
I have a band of tree brothers and sisters,
we are not melancholy babies.
I age like a rock, not a rocking chair.
A rock does not wear spectacles,
have a heart with winter in it,
or use a walking stick. It is dangerous
for anyone to call me "young fellow."

Happiness

One foot on the ground, I steal
what I love from a wordy wilderness,
I don't rob banks or make dirty deals,
no pickpocket I steal words, your happiness
without taking away your happiness.
I might name a dog Happy but not Happiness.
I peek in on two lovers tethered,
reading, writing, bathing together,
happy opposites and birds of a feather.

Happiness is tongues playing follow the leader
doing unto others as you
would have others do unto you.
I offer shelter to homeless readers.
I still have my voice but I cannot whistle.
Happiness perks my lips so I can whistle
a tune with Irish propinquity. The Irish
can't speak a word that is not musical.

Unhappiness has a certain authenticity.
The moon and sun are family, darkness
belongs to you and me,
the day belongs to no one, the night is ours.
I am frightened sometimes, family history:
I'll be hit by an armchair or bamboo.
I wake up in the morning with nothing to do
feed animals, write, water the flowers.
Now is the glorious spring of my content,
I will settle for sorrow and contentment.
Felicity, how now pretty lady. Happiness
is a Goddess in China, good news in Ghent,
I steal happiness, impossible flying elephant.

Christmas 2019

God rest you merry gentlemen,
may something you dismay.
14,000 sheep died on a capsized ship,
14,000 transported in the hold
from Romania, sold to Saudi Arabia,
sounds like slavery.
A sheep weighs 130 pounds,
a lamb less. I eat lamb and mutton
but I'm proud I never killed a lamb.
Slave children weigh less than sheep,
were priced less. I did not say "priceless."
Our Civil War cost 700,000 dead,
who fought over slavery, not sheep.
Without slaves, runaways and free
African-American regiments
no Appomattox: the North wouldn't have won.
Later, thanks to the lie the Spanish sank the Maine
there was reason to pocket Cuba, Hawaii, the Philippines,
bittersweet colonization, sugar wars.

When I was a disobedient black lamb,
Sugar Ray Robinson was champion
boxer. Beautiful and brave, he fought back
with employed and unemployed, women and men,
against tanks with their cannon pointing north
at Harlem, Malcolm X and Mohammed Ali.
Rioters filed out of churches and mosques
after services, after prayers on different days,
the homeless the stoned, the hallucinating, and Lady Day.
It was dangerous for every black to have one foot trapped
in hell, the same for black artists, writers, poets,
a long list of heroes. Looters broke windows,

stole what they needed: TVs, refrigerators,
what they could sell on the street in a hurry.
I forgot whites owned the stores, sometimes the prisons.
Invisible barbed wire for kids walking south
from their nation. Cool going anywhere nearby,
blacks turned
every few yards to see who was following.

Lost in the wilderness of misunderstanding,
I saw blue sunflowers and blue roses.
We all have the right to sing the blues.
"A rose by any other name would smell as sweet."
A slave is not a rose. Masters, why not write
a poem simple or complex with notes
how slavery still stinks! My darlings describe
whiffs of regretted improvements, battles
for voting rights, the stink of prenatal care,
take to the laundry of your soul
the lives of men and women for Christ's sake
hiding their tears, the whip of no salt
on the table in certain prisons.

In God we trust. 75% of Congress
represents 10% of the population.
Old times in the land of cotton,
are not forgotten. New thoughts are born
after a few New Orleans hot licks.
You who consider yourselves good eggs,
scrambled or hard boiled,
it's somewhere in the middle of the night.
Awake now, thinking and urinating, I remember
according to Darwin, to survive, everything fought
with everything. Today in Africa, 70%
of the population is under 30.

50% unemployed think and dream
with nothing to do. Africa's fertile land is becoming
desert in a hurry. The rivers and oceans
are rising, flooding again with no ark.
It's somewhere in the middle of the night.
I'll see what my scribbling looks like
7 a.m. on a happy Christmas day.

A Touch

There's too much writing
that is not about anything.
I walk in the woods of misunderstanding,
I see foxes chasing rabbits,
wild history and habits.
I find chanterelles and telephone
lines to the unknown.
I'm taken by frankness and disguise
of a woman with beautiful eyes,
the theatre of the soul.
They have a leading role
in a play, before the heart is broken
or a word spoken.
Without doubt, the curtain falls—
there are no curtain calls.
Today I walk on thin ice,
the not about anything,
I cross out the precise,
still seeming and feigning
have precise meanings.
I write with a touch of the unsaid,
meaning that is not read.
I'm thankful and grateful the moon is bright.
I'm grateful there's no moon tonight.

Tuning Up
    To Ellen Taaffe Zwilich

I discover and I salute Guido D'Arezzo
who invented musical notation
because singers failed
to remember Gregorian chants,
a new technique for teaching
ut-re-me-fa-so-la mnemonic.
I am going to write words
to pre-existing music
my song's meter
determined by the composer,
my feelings and thinking
full of unanswerable questions
my verse de-nationalized.
I'll make myself a refugee
writing songs.

For the love of Italy
my closeted love of China,
I'll tap my rosewood baton on the stand.
If you can't hear the *passato remoto*
in my voice listen to the cello,
my music determined poetry
that has little chance to rhyme.
What will I do for a piano and woodwinds,
my chance poetry?
I embrace you, we dance
but you choose every step.
Ellen, you don't compose chance or twelve-tone music.
The key in music demands
the first note in the piece is the same as the last.
Despite my purposes my various identities—I am.

Words for Ellen's Cello Concerto

A tenor needs a high C.
Devout and wild, the Christ Child
remembered the Red Sea.
A carpenter's son,
A boy, he taught lessons.
He grew from stable
to parables.
He invented history.
At Passover, his Last Supper they tell a story
around the table
they celebrate freedom from slavery.
The reason this night
is different from all other nights,

My Pathétique *is a gesture.*
Songbirds agree
every cello was once a tree.
Yes, "all the instruments
agree" an act of love may be a failure.
To set words to music may be a song,
an aria, beautiful and obscure
a concerto is a wordless song.
For most misery, music is the cure.
Goodnight, auf wiedersehen, *so long*
For my opera, Ellen, this is my overture.

Early Poem That Disappeared

Just before I got there, I toasted in Chinese
Ganbei. Dry cup. I've been to Lhasa, Tibet—
never-ending ice so thick the dead
are whispered prayers, lips close to the ear,
ritually butchered, then fed
to white-backed vultures screaming requiems.
To bathe at birth, marriage, and death
is not enough for me. Unteachable,
I knocked on the locked door of my imagination.
I smelled the stinking breath of my mortality.
I lifted a snapping turtle off Deerfield Road.
It bit into my shoe. I fell back
into a crabgrass ditch. I broke my right ankle
and left elbow. It was Memorial Day, a day
I broke my veteran bones on three occasions.
What do I know that no one knows?
I write a song that begins
"I fall back from making love
to the kind of day it is."
I lived to sing to my dying mother
from beside her bed. Now, memory is my mother.
I cannot escape the jail of poetry,
books books books books not stone.
I can throw myself away like a child's top
on a string, turn red and blue, then whirl
into a single color. Love came into my cell,
is jailed with me. A lady's absence
keeps her in my prison without a word.

Poem With Two Titles
*The Cooking Next Door Said Fish and Cabbage**

There's recitative and *Gespräch* music,
talk music, *Pierrot Lunaire*,
12-tone music you may compare
with this wordy trick:

COOKING

Why don't I understand what smells say today, said years ago,
what the sweet-smelling Last Supper said to the saintly diners
stench does not say dirty green words, thoughts smell,
words smell depending on what's happening:
age, garbage, and cabbage smell,
given what's cooking on language's stove.
Laila tov, that is "good night" in Hebrew,
smells beautiful to say. Lord, "good night"
has different smells and meanings.
Next, the ocean says "The earth will sink,"
the surf says "surprise demise, surprise demise."
Frankincense in churches comes from holy words,
the Beatitudes. I think I just heard a dove
smelling of incense coo *liberté, liberté.*
Songs also smell. Kitchen gardens are arguments.
Opera house dressing rooms smell of tights and sweaty brassieres,
a whiff says, "curtains and penises going up."

The language of smells is difficult for me to learn as Chinese.
I think I heard a flower or bee say, "love me,"
I put my foolish head in a rosebush for affection,
the Lord gave me a face of thorns.
Best to ask a child why the lilac bush said to the violets
"We are all ancestors, blooms."

I think I heard the smell of an ocean say, "remember."
I know a perfumed lady whose smell said, "father me" or "follow me."
Her hair whispered, *"Ich liebe dich."* I asked the smell of her hair
why it spoke German. "I'm braided with Goethe," her reply.
I understood, but I want to smell like Lorca.
Truth is, my father's family was pre-Iberic.
The River Nile flows, says she smells like Nefertiti,
lotus, and delta drek.
A girl passed me on the street, her smell mumbled something
in a language I did not understand. Her smell was angry.
That was yesterday, today I smell of something beyond
or before understanding, almost nothing.
Any listening smell can call me a "not quite."

Rivers and sonnets smell of copulation and onomatopoeia.
Still, I heard Amazon and Hudson talk
full of long vowel sounds and dialects.
A friend told me he saw a smell dance.
I said it must have been in the brothels of Argentina
that smell of tangos and Carlos Gardel.
My very own smell says, "underarm,
I'm bread in the oven, croissant in the crotch."

*Michael Schmidt

Not Reading or Writing, Waiting

Not reading or writing, waiting
for luncheon guests, I consider
my fish soup cooked in Riverdale, the Bronx
is not zuppa di pesce along the Arno.
Grownups don't tuck napkins under their chins.
In Dante's time, there was the gold florin,
Saint John on one side, the fleur-de-lis on the other.
Guelphs vs. Ghibellines, Emperor vs. Pope,
afterwards eye vs. telescope.
Germans bombed the Ponte Santa Trinita.
Who will be next to die, is anyone expecting a baby?

My guests are late, students I've never met.
Politically, I support a parliament of fish,
They follow the leader without question.
Fish are pagan, I never hooked a Christian fish,
but Jesus was a guide on the Saint Lawrence.
I believe I must have paddled, rowed,
motored over Christian fish, lords, and commoners.
I keep the rule of medieval host to guest,
guest to host, the importance of medieval names,
da, to give, short for Dante, that was Durante.
I don't expect to hear loud belches at lunch,
appreciation after fasting.

Since my dogs are not here today,
who shall I feed under the table?
Under the table, wherever I sit, ghosts of my dogs—
Horatio, Sancho, Dulci (Dulcinea),
Daisy (Montauk Daisy), Luke,
Zoopie (Zeus), Velvet, Rhumba,
Nicky, Honey, and still alive, Margie.

I'm forgetting a dog, he or she is outside, lonely,
I daydream. *The cook, he was scalded*
for all his long ladle. I unlock the door.
Outside above my door, a two-faced
marble god, Janus, god of beginnings,
guardian of passageways and doors,
his young face looks at a happy future,
his old bearded face searches the past.
It's a beautiful January day,
named after the god of civilization.

Unknown Reason For

I'm sorry I was afraid
to hold a six-week-old baby.
I have essential tremor. Nothing
is quite safe in my hands.
"Essential" means, medically,
"unknown reason for." I've a history,
I hold parts of someone
firmly in hand, but not
a 13-pound baby, the last pound
recently acquired. I have no problem
kissing his head. I asked
his grandmother of five children
to hold him. She asked me to bless the child.
I'm sure Joseph had no problem
holding the Christ child.
I've put fallen swallows
gently back
into their nests. I could make a list
of my fears. Top of the list
begins with the letter D.
I'd rather no one says "I'm sorry,
but he had a good life," my soul
sent special delivery
in an unaddressed envelope.

Scuttlebutt

I was sleepless and afraid to sleep.
I could sleep on a haystack of barbed wire,
on anybody's fat-ass pillow.
What was *was*, what is *is*.
In the US Navy, I was Seaman Third Class,
my shipmate, last name "Love," asked me to write
a letter to his girlfriend in popular songs.
I wrote, "I'll see you in apple blossom time."
Killed, his head was bloody applesauce.
He did not die for no reason, or any metaphor.
His cause: the right to love and pub crawl
along the old Bowery under the elevated trains,
drunk, the right to stroll, fall, get up.
He protected the rights of others
to cross-dress on the Way of the Cross.

On a wall, in a notebook, in museums and libraries,
I have confused heaven and art.
I've seen an artist in residence, an ant
carrying a breadcrumb to an anthill.
If there's a God, He moves in mysterious ways.
Will a deaf ant be given equal justice by God
with Johann Sebastian Bach playing Fugues
and Preludes in brick Lutheran churches?
The wish to give and receive is necessary
as breathing in and breathing out.
Heart beats, regular and irregular, are heaven sent.
My heartbeat is allegro staccato,
whereas my kidney and liver are agnostic.
Friends of my kidney, are there bodies, factories,
fields, rivers, working places, beds in paradise?

Love love love, love so desperate
I met a lover who fucked, he said, the cavity
of a raw chicken, plucked. He would not tell
if it was hen, rooster, or metaphor.
I've also tried to oversleep history,
the idea of a dead body. *170 pounds*
of cold meat, four buckets of water, a pocket of salt.
Suicide is throwing your cell phone in the Thames.

Manservant

Death, you are God's manservant,
ordered not to observe the Sabbath:
Seven days thou shalt labor,
thou shalt kill every living thing,
thou shalt steal from every living thing,
thou shalt show no mercy to any living thing,
thou shalt take the Lord's name in vain,
thou shalt marry thy dead self,
thou shalt covet thy neighbor's wife, daughter, and son.
Commit adultery with thyself!
Proud, thou shalt not die
because thou servest the Lord.
Thou wast the servant of the Word,
thou heldest back the light from darkness.
Death, you dwell among us. I believe
I heard the Lord say "Yes, for good reasons."

Happy Holiday

We have never spent a birthday
or holiday together. Let's try
for next Thanksgiving, or Angel's birthday.
We are not family but we are brothers.
Mom's love of life, Papa's poetry, you
a Christian Jew like Jesus, I a Jew
trying with all the might I've left
to do more than I can to set the universe right.
In Grand Central and Petersfield Station
I polish the shoes of history.
I climb a green willow,
wave the future toward us,
mounted on a lame horse
or loaded in a truck with three flat tires.

I never heard a silent birthday party.
When was Hamlet's birthday?
I cast my good eye on life and death.
I'm on trial like Kafka,
I'm a witness, judge and grand jury.
The charge is perjury. I deny
the ugly truth that hurts. You say "Enough of that."
A kiss is a better invention than anything
artificial intelligence will postulate.
A blown kiss has a certain togetherness.
I blow you a kiss across the Atlantic to Manchester.
It brings you closer.
I wish it were earlier than I think it is right now.
There's Heaven, but I don't believe death's a holiday.

My History of Laughter

My history of laughter:
the first human beings who laughed
were thrown out of their caves by grunters
and humpers because they wanted romance.
Chuckles and smiles. There must have been laughter
before marriage vows and last rites.
"We are the only mammals who laugh" is not true.
There are those who laugh a lot
because of too much grief.
Every living thing laughs.
Flowers laugh so hard their petals fall.
Gardens are sometimes like a theatre
with comic and tragic hydrangeas,
some roses have thorns.
I hear laughter, it's raining hard,
laughter after a hot summer day.
If you don't think maples, oaks, evergreens laugh,
walk in another part of the forest,
come sit with me under a greenwood tree.
I smile when I hear "War of the Roses," laugh
with the laughing birds: the green woodpeckers,
laughing thrush, laughing doves and crows.
I am a bird feeder, a laugh,
some birds hunt for dead men's teeth.

Beautiful to think in the beginning was the word
according to Matthew, according to Mark,
according to John, according to Luke. I play
the most Christian instrument: the accordion.
(I hear a little laughter in the pit). Further back,
when the Spirit of God moved on the face of the waters,
when God created the heavens and the earth

laughter came about the time there was light,
laughter and light were good. Jokes become comics.

> *Tonight, come and kiss me sweet and sixty,*
> *seventy, eighty, ninety.*
> *I sing a song of my devotion,*
> *I'm a little drunk, be my ocean,*
> *take me on a cruise*
> *around the world. Be my muse,*
> *show me poetry is not complaining,*
> *the truest poetry is the most feigning.*
> *Ocean, come over my bow, let's sail*
> *into the fog up ahead, the future.*
> *Kind winds prevail,*
> *there is no end, there is departure.*
> *Night comes. I sound a foghorn,*
> *I am reborn.*
> *I'm beginning to know who I am,*
> *I want. I give a damn.*
> *Darling ocean, sweet adventure,*
> *I am a gardener, a rake, the grand tour.*
> *Youth's a stuff will not endure.*

Wordsworth beheld "the sea lay laughing at a distance."
If water equals time, providing beauty with its double,
so be it. I keep time with water clocks,
Greek and Medieval candle clocks.
I know how to make a laughing clock:
ha, haha, hahaha, up to twelve.
I want this verse to be a laughing clock.
I have not forgotten the sun on water
is a ripple of laughter.
In a confession booth a sinner
laughed so piously he was given absolution.

He did not hail Mary, he laughed with her.
Freud on humor: A man about to be hanged
says, What a beautiful day for a hanging.

A newborn sinless babe does not laugh.
A world away from The Book of Proverbs,
the Japanese have a saying, "Letting off a fart
doesn't make you laugh when you are alone."
Idle reader, I never heard a snake break wind.
A rattlesnake did a twisting dance in my house.
I picked up the serpent with two sticks,
threw it into an apple tree. It didn't get the joke,
went off without enchantment in search of a charmer.

Here is my fairy tale, The Birthday Cake:
you take six eggs, beat the yolks and whites,
a little flour, half an hour in the oven.
Laughter. The batter rises,
strawberries and cream for shortcake.
A loving mother hen missed her eggs,
she jumped on top of the cake, sat on her beaten eggs,
wept on the pretty cake in the center of the table.
Outside in the yard a rooster mounted
a New Hampshire Red. The guests laughed.

I circled Manhattan with Pablo Neruda
on a ferry—Neruda, Communist rooster
on top of the world, dressed, it seemed,
in Savile Row tweed, Church's shoes. We talked.
He remembered under the Triboro Bridge,
"I asked Lorca to come with me to a circus:
old tightrope walkers and acrobats,
an old clown shot out of a cannon."
Lorca's answered a 1935 question

with an Andalusian frown that suffers in translation,
"Pablo, it's getting difficult. I must leave *España,*
go to Grenada to kiss the Lorcas and Romeros goodbye."
Federico was shot by unnecessary bullets
that whistled half notes and quarter notes.
He died at sunrise, not five o'clock
in the afternoon. Fascist laughter.

Present mirth has present laughter.
Buddha laughs with joy, thanks to the hereafter.
Someone shouts, "There is the laughter of murderers!
Nothing funnier than a dead body!"
It's worth repeating: *170 pounds of cold meat,*
four buckets of water, a pocket of salt.
I throw my sombrero into the Mediterranean.
It floats—mysterious laughter.
I can see Silenus laughing with Dionysus.
They drink laughing wine in dazzling goblets.
I can't forget Eros laughs with happy lovers
in cheap, dear rooms of Washington Heights.

I remember a Bernini fountain, in Piazza Navona,
water laughing, I drank out of the mouth of a satyr.
The satyr kissed me.
It was Epiphany, when shepherds come to Rome
from the *compagna,* playing goatskin bagpipes.
When I'm laid out, I prefer to keep my skin.
They can make a bagpipe fashioned of my laughing belly,
I'll be a musical instrument, I prefer
being blown than fingered like a harp or clavier.

I was moved to tears by a laughing jazz band,
black laughter instead of drums. Chick Webb could do it,
Louis Armstrong forced a scat-laugh revolution.

Laughter is ancient as the sun, older than the moon.
The Chinese word for laughter is made of two characters:
the character for sky beneath the character for grass.
Translated in Chinese a laughing Falstaff
might give you a dancing Falstaff tripping on a sunset,
upside down cows and sheep grazing in the sky.
What is the moon doing rising below my feet?
Laugh me to scorn.
"Weeping may endure all night,
but joy cometh in the morning."

Three

It was a dream.
      It took time for me
            to realize that.
I saw a beautiful girl,
      John Ashbery's wife, strolling.
            I told her, "I found out 3 days ago
there are butterflies with 3 wings.
      Don't tell John now
            I'm writing a poem
about the number 3."
      I woke,
            got things right—
John died 3 years ago.
      Still there are *The Three Sisters*
            and 3 blind mice.
Jonah was in the belly
      of the whale,
            3 days and 3 nights.
Leviticus, 3rd book in the Bible,
      teaches us to love our neighbor
            as our self.
There were the 3 questions
      Oedipus answered.
            Samuel had to be awakened 3 times.
Switzerland has 3 languages.
      In the old days, number 1 was urine,
            number 2 feces,
number 3, then and now, wasting time stinks.
      These lines hang like bunches of grapes.
            At the risk of my life,
I swam in the mythological
      rivers of Italy:
            the Tiber, the Arno, the Po.

I remember 3 wise men and God in 3 persons.
  I can't forget the 3 Marys,
    Mary of Egypt once a whore.
I love the trio in Rosenkavalier
  that begins with "Heut oder Morgen."
    Ladies have 3 openings that give pleasures.
At 3am and other times I've seen
    whites, mostly blacks, eat out of garbage cans,
      the homeless wandering.
Columbus sailed on 3 ships
  full of indentured servants,
    Jews, and Scarlet fever.
He did not get to India.
  He brought back to Europe
    with a little help
potatoes, tobacco,
  chocolate, slaves,
    monarch butterflies.
To the Chinese
  the number 3
    may still be
a dead ancestor.
  The number 3 is pretty,
    5 has a big belly.
What words rhyme or partially rhyme with 3,
  a happy mystery of butterflies' wings?
    333 6th Avenue
used to be New Directions' address.
  John, in my dream,
    would have been about 33.
I have not forgotten
  trilogies, triptychs, a ménage à trois,
    what Dante did with 3 lines.
In Spain, the 3 arches of Lorca,
  one with Muse, one with angel,
    one bare with nothing: *nada, el duende.*

I have not forgotten 333 or so death camps,
      perhaps butterflies understood
            so they grew a third wing.
I won't forget the races,
      the winner,
            place, and show.
I've tried to hit a homerun
      into the bleachers but this time
            I had 3 strikes, I'm out.

Pasture

I will never be put out to pasture.
My old horses are put out to pasture,
some old horses are sold for dog food,
I feed dogs, share my food with them.
I might be meat for grizzlies if I stumble
into a nest of cubs. I have some memory
of sailors starving in a dory, drawing lots,
the loser: human steaks.
I will never be put out to pasture
long as I have something to say about it.
When I feed my opera-loving donkeys,
they bray: *Stay with us. Stay with us.*
I live in the country, that compared
to the city, where I lived as a child,
is "out to pasture." Some have drunk
to others only with their eyes.
I drink and graze on Irish daisies that grow
in the countryside, and steel-girdled
cemented cities with my eyes. I want
all things in nature to ride my back.
The oceans are lighter than mountains,
I don't rear up, buck them off,
I am happy with my burden. Old horse,
I do not want to die fallen in a stall,
it's better outside, unhitched, halter dangling,
trying to get up on my own four legs.

Now I am just a man, not a metaphor.
I say to myself: Here I am.
I see a ram, horns caught in a thicket—
I free the ram, my hands bleed from thorns.
I do not believe sacrifice is a good cause.

I make a fire that warms me, it's not a burnt offering,
I have no favorite son.
I will not lay a hand on anyone,
except to comfort her or him.
I am grateful I can rest a while
in the kindness of green and rocky pastures.

Resemblance

I could write a poem all remembrance. I try to speak
the truth of remembrance, far from a lie as I can get.
Walking with the truth, I stroll with one foot
the God's honest truth, limping with the other.
Truth is a breed of dog or cat that has resemblances,
a face has resemblances, not the soul.

Age 17, a sailor, too young to drink at a bar,
I had a double whiskey in Hoboken, went to war.
Twenty days at sea from the Jersey dock to Plymouth,
I was an armed guard on a freighter, Simms,
manned a 20 millimeter, not much of a gun
against German subs. Stevens' *Harmonium* was in my hammock,
food and ammunition in the hold. In my notebook,
by mistake, I first spelled *guard*, God.
I remember mountain-high Atlantic waves.
I was frightened by the blue, green, and white.
The ship would fall back down a water cliff, then down
a little more forward than back, but not always.
Any minute a torpedo might explode the ship. I was on duty
four hours on, four hours off, hours added to duty
for good reason, never extra duty off. Off duty I wrote
hopeful lines in ink (we were much closer
to the angel of death than ball-point pens).

77 years later, COVID-19—the world
is a ship on the ocean surrounded by German subs.
I remember my wild boyhood feelings.
Now I am with my cargo of books,
my wife, my friends, and all strangers I love.
77 years ago, most sentences contained the word *fucking*.
"Pass the fucking salt." I remember a tough-guy shipmate

weeping with terror and wetting his hammock.
Sometimes he fucked the hammock under him. I wept
when we arrived in Plymouth
the first time I heard English English.
Shakespeare, Milton, and Donne were on our side.
I thought it was 50-50 I'd make it, but we'll win.
Roosevelt and Churchill were on the radio, I laughed
listening to Axis Sally. I never believed in Santa Claus.
How much destruction can a malignant psychopath cause?

Pandemic: Wear Gloves and a Mask

Obscene, undemocratic,
his army condemned before battle,
tonight, death in a cape,
a king disguised,
strolls among humanity.
The innocent touch him without gloves.
I feel a touch of death, my acquaintance
perhaps a neighbor
I call him Sir or Lady in the night.
In the doorknob now
that once held a smiling angel,
almost faceless, the smiling angel of death.

Pratfall

I want to write a doggerel farce,
part carousel, part kick in the arse.
My donkeys, Melody and Prosody,
when the radio plays Bach or Puccini,
heehaw, heehaw, heehaw, bray in rhyme.
Like them I want to have a real good time.

Rhyme is sexual, a word that wants another word's
sound, a reach, an embrace, sometimes absurd,
often beautiful, free to be unfaithful, or in stanza form
that may be late revolutionary or conform:
sonnets, villanelles, tablets in cuneiform.

Birdsong is public education.
An American song may be conversation
with a lover or dead relation.
From time to time there is the temptation,
when loneliness is lost in fire,
there's the desire
to lift the coffin lid, to see what dying did,
or you can drill a little hole,
peek in, assist at *Grand Guignol.*
Looking at departed mothers,
fathers, brothers, sisters, others,
proves every death's a dandy liar.
Death undresses for dinner, changes attire,
after the ball is over.
They had a good time crossing over
the straits of Dover,
crossing the Styx in 1066.
History is now a farce, a play,
you are a supernumerary.

Aristophanes rhymed. Plato said,
Frogs, *Wasps*, and *Clouds* mirrored Athen's face.
It's wonderful to be alive or dead,
never to be born is a disgrace.

Back to the beginning, James Joyce
had conversation with Ibsen. *Exiles*
did not rhyme with *Ghosts* or *Wild Duck*.
Guardian angels in Oslo and Dublin still rejoice.
Despite changing currencies,
the angels love the same godly trees.
A Celtic or Baltic mother is good luck,
two eggs in one nest, beauty and duty.
Joyce refused his mother's last wish
that he observe his Easter duties.
The world is grateful for wild Irish
wisdom, beauty, and much more. When Åse died,
Peer Gynt found his secret bride.
Two great eggs were turned over, scrambled and fried.
The English language was freed from the prison
of sentences. Good stilly night. The agreed
and disagreement of metaphors flourished
for the undernourished –
there was a book to read all their lives. It was good,
Finnegan celebrated the death of you understood,
an enchanting misunderstanding.
Come and kiss me, sweet Miss Understanding.
The meanings of a word
battle everywhere for their right to be heard.
A word is a nest of rattlesnakes in Uxmal,
where words are skulls on a limestone wall,
where a ring on a rattlesnake's skin is a New Year.
'I love you' may mean come here.

In Firenze's café Santo Spirito
try the *osso buco*, don't forget the marrow.
A vineyard protects an injured sparrow,
the Buddha enlightens the world, has big ears.
God's eyes are on the sparrow,
He also hears.
Chaos has a voice,
Babel was His choice.
He is awash, more than baptized,
He is often advised
by wildflowers. The least
among us is the most prized.
A mouthful of grass can be a feast.
The Lord knows the difference
between fact and fiction.
I guess he prefers fiction
after beginnings and verbs,
Psalms and Proverbs.
Death's just a barbed-wire fence –
leap over or crawl under.
Lightning is human, so is thunder.
God is wonder.
Every living thing can wonder.

Ode to an Antique Boy

1.
Before I shaved I remember
I was impossibly ancient.
I did not give in, surrender
to myself. It was my fate
to be a city state. I would separate
armies within me, with a guarded gate:
the wounded and never healing,
lovers with opposite feelings,
their naked bodies blessed with kisses.
I quarreled with myself. I would insist
I take a look how the living pissed.
Man and boy pissed a fountain
different from my pissing fountain.
Some dogs peed with one leg up
I wondered why some almost sat down,
why in my trousers the perpetual lump.
I loved the country, not the town,
the holidays within me, not the clock.
I knew time wasn't tick-tock
when I listened to and saw what was
under a lady's silent dressing gown.
I worshipped the mysterious, the hair,
what I barely saw was up there.
Yes, there was confusion, a touch of illusion
in my state, my provinces, my body,
my grammar, my body parts, my reasoning,
my out of mind reasoning.
I hoped that I would
understand the wisdom of others,
God in three persons,
brothers who understood the brotherhood
of everyone.

2.

Since childhood I broke the rules,
rules of the road and games.
I was game and wild game
chased by a wolf, myself. My wolf's muzzle
was something like a crossword puzzle.
I found I, we, us,
this and that, ambiguous.
I'm a dancing monkey with a cup.
I won't surrender to death, that is a hiccup.
Life is always womanly.
Death, an unwanted guest, is manly.
I slap death in the face.
Death turns the other cheek.
I slap death in the face.
Death turns the other cheek.

I jump over the fences of language,
meter is not a cage.
When I'm in my coffin
I'll slap death in the face.
Death's not a Christian
invented by the Lord.
Death's a hiccup, a trip abroad.
After the flood
there was a bastard dove, a rainbow
high in the clouds; now it's low
I can almost touch God's
multi-colored eyebrow.

Margie and Honey in full face and profile

ALSO BY STANLEY MOSS

Almost Complete Poems
Seven Stories Press, Carcanet Press Ltd.

God Breaketh Not All Men's Hearts Alike: New and Selected Poems (1948-2019)
Carcanet Press Ltd.

It's About Time
Hopewell Press, Carcanet Press Ltd.

No Tear is Commonplace
Carcanet Press Ltd.

God Breaketh Not All Men's Hearts Alike (2007)
Seven Stories Press

Rejoicing
Carcanet Press Ltd., Anvil Press Poetry Ltd.

Songs of Imperfection
Carcanet Press Ltd., Anvil Press Poetry Ltd.

A History of Color
Seven Stories Press

August Follies: satyr song, a poem, and prose parables
Privately Printed

Asleep in the Garden
Seven Stories Press, Carcanet Press Ltd., Anvil Press Poetry Ltd.

The Intelligence of Clouds
Harcourt Brace Jovanovich, Carcanet Press Ltd., Anvil Press Poetry Ltd.

Skull of Adam
Horizon Press, Carcanet Press Ltd., Anvil Press Poetry Ltd.

The Wrong Angel
Macmillan, Carcanet Press Ltd., Anvil Press Poetry Ltd.

Gedichte
translated by Hans Magnus Enzensberger, Hanser

Selected Poems
translated by Fu Hao, Chongqing University Press

Ya Era Hora
translated by Valerie Mejer, Syracuse University Press

PRAISE FOR STANLEY MOSS

"Stanley Moss creates poems that grow far grander than the usual attempts to congeal one's inner life with natural or artificial worlds. Instead, this writing projects a sense of connectedness among private histories, personal mythologies, and public loves that clearly transcends the poet and his basic purpose. Here is a mind operating in open air, unimpeded by fashion or forced thematic focus, profoundly catholic in perspective, at once accessible and erudite, inevitably compelling. All of which is to recommend Moss's ability to participate in and control thoroughly these poems while resisting the impulse to center himself in them. This differentiates this compelling work from much contemporary breast-beating . . . The language here is both simple and aspiring, the rhythms natural yet elegant. Throughout, readers are in sight—and sound—of an accomplished, assuring voice. On a personal level, Moss's voice codifies and dramatizes lament, as in this articulation of grief for his mother's passing in 'For Margaret':

> My mother near her death
> is white as a downy feather.
> I used to think her death was
> as distant as a tropical bird,
> a giant macaw, whatever that is
> —a thing I have as little to do with
> as the distant poor.
> I find a single feather of her suffering.
> I blow it gently as she blew
> into my neck and ear.

Moss stands equally comfortable whether summoning the resources of a thirteenth-century Hebrew poet, or crafting a letter to butterflies, or focusing on the realization of his mother's death, or fictionalizing a comic romp with Lenin and Gorky, or considering the specter of Hannibal and his brilliant elephants, or recollecting a spring in Beijing. Moss is an artist who embraces the possibilities of exultation, appreciation, reconciliation, of extreme tenderness. As such he lays down a commitment to a common, worldly morality toward which all beings gravitate. More, reading Moss,

you get a true tingle for a sense of life universal, and that is indeed a rare prize among the many offerings of contemporary American poetry."
—**G.F. Murray,** *American Book Review*

"'Death is a many-colored harlequin,' asserts Stanley Moss on his 92nd birthday. Undaunted, outrageously alive, Moss in these Abandoned Poems flaunts more colors than the Grim Reaper ever dreamed of, laughs in his face, rhymes with abandon, makes a joyful noise unto the Lord, and struts with Baudelaire. This is a book to hold onto for dear life."
—**Rosanna Warren**

"As grand in his generosity as he is in his appetites . . . the larger-than-life persona Moss has created and sustained is good to have in your head, and at your side. God may or may not be his co-pilot, but Moss has a knack for lifting my spirits into 'the sweaty / life-loving, Book-loving air of happiness.'"
—**Parnassus**

"Stanley Moss is oceanic: his poems rise, crest, crash, and rise again like waves. His voice echoes the boom of the Old Testament, the fluty trill of Greek mythology, and the gongs of Chinese rituals as he writes about love, nature, war, oppression, and the miracle of language. He addresses the God of the Jews, of the Christians, and of the Muslims with awe and familiarity, and chants to lesser gods of his own invention. In every surprising poem every song to life, beautiful life, Moss, by turns giddy and sorrowful, expresses a sacred sensuality and an earthy holiness. Or putting it another way: here is a mind operating in open air, unimpeded by fashion or forced thematic focus, profoundly catholic in perspective, at once accessible and erudite, inevitably compelling. All of which is to recommend Moss's ability to participate in and control thoroughly these poems while resisting the impulse to center himself in them. This differentiates his beautiful work from much contemporary breast-beating. Moss is an artist who embraces the possibilities of exultation, appreciation, reconciliation, of extreme tenderness. As such he lays down a commitment to a common, worldly morality toward which all beings gravitate."
—**Donna Seaman**